PRAISE FOR *JESUS UNPLUGGED*

In this book Bert Gary pres[ents] power to shock his contempora[ry] our easy assurances and smo[ ] him seriously. Such a fresh encounter can unleash the transforming power of the Gospel in our time and in our church. Amen and bravo!

—James Laney
President Emeritus–Emory University

Let's face it, Jesus unsettled people. So does this book. Jesus challenged people to let go of their security blankets and meet God face-to-face. So does this book. Jesus pulled no punches. Neither does this book.

—John Rosemond
Family psychologist, syndicated parenting columnist, and best-selling author, www.rosemond.com

Dorothy Sayers used to complain that Christians have attempted to domesticate the Lion of Judah, and she was right. We've worked hard to create a Jesus in our own image, one who was above all else a really nice guy. Bert Gary exposes the fabrication and challenges our longings for a tamed Lord. If you're ready for the veneer to be peeled away, then read this book, but beware ... the real Jesus has not been declawed.

—Rev. Cary Stockett
Senior Pastor–Christ United Methodist Church
Jackson, Mississippi

Many who are quoting scripture and preaching the gospel are perpetuating half truths. Bert Gary, with a robust but reverent boldness plumbs the depths of the mind of Christ—revealing the whole truth that makes us free indeed.

—L. Bevel Jones
United Methodist Bishop (Retired)–Development Office
Candler School of Theology–Emory Universty

Jesus Unplugged is a creative invitation for all of us to look with fresh eyes and open hearts at many of the sayings and teachings of Jesus. In his own unique, thought-provoking, and soul-stirring way, Bert Gary has opened some of the Gospel lessons for us who live in this postmodern world. Drawing on the work of Edwin Friedman and connecting them with sayings of Jesus, we are brought into a helpful conversation that can provide insights into leadership and discipleship in the 21st century. In good Friedman fashion, Bert has disturbed the system and challenged us to faithfulness and obedience to Jesus.

—Bishop Larry M. Goodpaster
Alabama–West Florida Conference
The United Methodist Church

Jesus Unplugged is for seekers who are strong and brave enough to want to meet Jesus, face to face. Excellent for groups—youth, young adults, adults—who want to be challenged to move beyond assumptions and polite conversation. The "Unplug Your Mind" questions are superb: Much discussion will be engendered as they are posed. Read *Jesus Unplugged* and your spiritual life will grow deeper and wider as you unplug from preconception and move toward honest engagement with the Savior of All.

Jesus Unplugged is a must for youth groups, campus ministry groups, adult Sunday School classes, growth groups. Discover the adventure of life with the Jesus who is divinely provocative and infinitely fascinating and powerfully redeeming.

—Bishop Hope Morgan Ward
Mississippi Conference
The United Methodist Church

PROVOCATIVE,

RAW AND FULLY EXPOSED

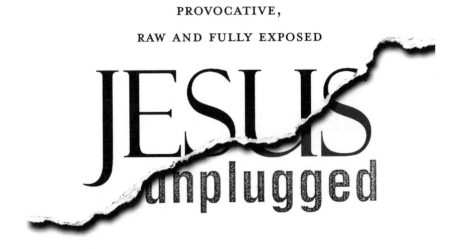

JESUS unplugged

BERT GARY

FaithWalk
PUBLISHING
Grand Haven, Michigan

Published by FaithWalk Publishing
Grand Haven, Michigan 49417

The Scripture versions cited in this book are identified in Appendix 1, which hereby becomes a part of this copyright page.

Printed in the United States of America
10 09 08 07 06 05   7 6 5 4 3 2 1

Library of Congress Cataloging-in-Publication Data

Gary, Bert.
Jesus unplugged : provocative, raw, and fully exposed / by Bert Gary.-- 1st ed.
    p. cm.
Includes bibliographical references and index.
ISBN-13: 978-1-932902-54-9 (pbk. : alk. paper)
ISBN-10: 1-932902-54-6
1. Jesus Christ—Character. I. Title.
BT304.G37 2005
232.9'03—dc22

                    2005020392

DEDICATION

Though Rabbi Friedman died in October of 1996, his work continues to influence leaders of all faiths. He released *Generation to Generation*, his foundational text, in 1985. In 1990, his delightfully subversive *Friedman's Fables* was published. Finally, *A Failure of Nerve: Leadership in the Age of the Quick Fix* was published in 2000, the culmination of over a decade of lectures on leadership. His genius was in taking Dr. Murray Bowen's family system therapy concepts and applying them broadly yet precisely to churches, synagogues, businesses, and even governments. Friedman's books, various video and audio tapes of his lectures, and notes taken at his seminars have contributed to this book.

Upon my first introduction to the work of Rabbi Friedman, an internal conversation began. Friedman and Jesus began to talk. That was 1993. The conversation took on a life of its own. As it turned out, that conversation in my head was this book's conception and gestation. It was born in a 4-week period of intense late night and early morning typing binges. It took its present form after a few years of road testing with helpful friends, ministerial classes, Sunday school classes, and Bible studies (and a good publisher).

I went to one of Dr. Friedman's seminars in Atlanta exactly one year before his death. We shook hands during a break. Leaning on the table next to his overhead projector, he was a taller man than I expected, and I told him I appreciated all his work. He was cordial, nodding, smiling the weak smile of a person who gets thanked a lot.

Once again I find I owe him my thanks. So it should be no surprise that I dedicate this book to the memory of Rabbi Edwin H. Friedman.

CONTENTS

PREFACE

A ccording to the four Gospels of the New Testament, Jesus was raised in a small village called Nazareth, in a region called Galilee, in Roman-occupied first century Palestine. His ministry began when he was about thirty years old (Lk 3:23). Jesus's life ended when he was no younger than thirty-six, contrary to popular opinion that Jesus died at the age of exactly thirty-three. Thirty-three is calculated using two questionable assumptions: one, that "about thirty" means exactly thirty (Lk 3:23); and two, that since John's Gospel mentions three Passover festivals Jesus attended (Jn 2:13, 5:1, 13:1), one can assume that he attended exactly three and no more. 30+3=33. Good math. Bad conclusion.

How old was Jesus when he died? We may never know exactly. But, the Gospels give just enough details that, assuming their historical record of events is accurate, we can hazard a guess at his age and be within five years either way.

Matthew 2:1 says that Jesus was born during the reign of Herod the Great; Herod died in 4 B.C. So Jesus must have been born before 4 B.C. The first Gospel also says that in an unknown year Herod learned from Magi that a Judean king of the lineage of David may have been born within the past two years prior to their visit from the East (Mt 2:2, 7, and 16). Magi (singular is *magos* in Greek) is the root for our English word magician. Two or more of them are said by Matthew to have studied a star of some interest to them for two years. This unusual celestial event led them to believe that a new king had been born in Judah. Astronomy and astrology were common areas of study for Magi. They were not so much "kings" or "wise men" as they were a prophet-like class of scholarly astrologers and dream interpreters; sometimes they are described as magicians or sorcerers (Acts 8:9,11; 13:6, 8); they studied religious and secular knowledge.

To repeat, the Magi of Matthew's Gospel believed the new king of Israel's birth to have happened about two years prior to their arrival in Jerusalem, because that was when they first saw his star. Whatever that star might have been, they learned in Jerusalem that a great king was expected by Jewish prophesy to be born in Bethlehem, just six miles south of Jerusalem (Mt 2:3–8). Consequently, after the Magi escaped from Bethlehem, Herod ordered all the children in Bethlehem *two-years-old and under* to be killed (Mt 2:16).

So the Magi went to Bethlehem and visited the *toddler* and his mother in "the house" (Mt 2:11). The Magi did not go to the manger the night of Jesus's birth, but two years later they arrived at the home in which Jesus's family lived in Bethlehem. Both the Magi and Jesus's family escaped Herod's wrath (Mt 2:12–14). The Magi went home. The family went to Egypt and did not return until after Herod the Great's death in 4 B.C. (Mt 2:15).

Based on this, Jesus was born in 6 B.C. at the absolute *latest*; that would be 4 B.C. plus the two years the Magi watched the star equals 6 B.C. If then Jesus died in 30 A.D.—the *earliest* possible date for his crucifixion—then he was at least thirty-six when he died. Yet Jesus could have been born as early as 12 B.C. and crucified as late as 33 A.D. That would make him forty-five when he died, which interestingly was about the life expectancy for adult males in first century Israel.

This makes Jesus's age at his time of death thirty-six to forty-five. The midway point between those two ages is forty-and-a-half. But that's not the point. The important thing here is that this age range makes Jesus older than the accepted thirty-three. Is there other scriptural evidence that Jesus could have been forty-ish when he died? Absolutely.

The other reference in Scripture to Jesus's age can be found in John 8:57. Opponents said to him, "You are not yet fifty years old." This statement suggests—and the time-line supports it—that Jesus was in his forties when he was executed by the Romans by means of what they called "the ultimate penalty"—crucifixion.

But what does Jesus's age have to do with exposing his provocative message? Think about it. Jesus was no young firebrand snuffed out in his tender years. He was no rookie. Rather, he was a mature elder of the people and a seasoned veteran of biblical and theological study and debate. Even at the tender age of twelve Jesus demonstrated advanced understanding (Lk 2:46–47). Imagine what he was capable of at forty!

A reasonable theory is that Jesus's ministry started when he was in his early thirties, beginning in a kind of partnership with John the Baptist (Jn 3:22–30; Jn 4:1–3). After John's death, Jesus made his center of operation the town of Capernaum, where he was said to be "at home," (Mk 1:14, 2:1) and from where he called full-time disciples and launched a full-time ministry. He went from Jewish village to Jewish village teaching and healing. He went on the required annual pilgrimages to the temple in Jerusalem with his disciples. He sent many disciples out on missionary journeys to surrounding regions. He gained an enormous following. Jesus also made numerous enemies, including Galilee's king, a son of Herod the Great named Herod Antipas. As Jesus neared the end of his ministry, in his late thirties or early forties, his notoriety became a threat to his safety.

That is the big picture. But there is a critical moment described in Chapter 9 of the Gospel of Luke, verse 51. Jesus had left Galilee, going north into the region ruled by Herod Philip, the brother of Herod Antipas. The two kings were not on good terms (Mk 6:17), so Jesus was safer with Philip who, so far as we know, never knew or sought Jesus of Nazareth. Fleeing Galilee because of the threat of arrest by Antipas and a number of pressures to be revealed in Chapter 4, Jesus prayed and discussed his future with his disciples in Philip's capital of Caesarea Philippi (Mt 16:13; Mk 8:27). There Jesus taught the disciples for the first time that he must be killed. That was his destiny. But they did not understand. Moreover, one of his closest disciples, Simon Peter, did not approve of this plan, and he may not have been alone (Mt 16:22; Mk 8:32). Think about it. Getting yourself killed doesn't sound like a very good idea on the face of it, does it? And Simon Peter told him so. But Jesus was undeterred. At a critical turning point, Jesus set off toward Jerusalem knowing that there he would be killed.

Jesus has made some powerful enemies along the way, as we shall see. He is heading into the furnace of Jerusalem's hate and plotting, and he knows it. This destiny is the background for everything else that happens on the way to the capital, including the episode in Luke 12 in which two brothers interrupt Jesus's teaching to get him to settle their squabble over an inheritance. Yes, inheritances are important. But Jesus is marching to his death, and Luke does not want us to miss the terrible irony of his having to stop and deal with comparatively trivial matters like the settling of an estate. He is going to his death, and two unnamed brothers are obsessed with a few bucks. That is the backdrop of the following story. And Jesus's destiny in Jerusalem also happens to be the backdrop and destination of this book.

ACKNOWLEDGMENTS

Much appreciation to the following persons:

- To those who read this book
- To Dirk Wierenga, Jenn Phipps, Ginny McFadden, and Louann Werksma of FaithWalk Publishing
- To Jim Laney, John Rosemond, Leonard Sweet, Hope Morgan Ward, Larry Goodpaster, Baxter Kruger, Bev Jones, and Cary Stockett (who is also in Perichoresis and the Brothers of the Bread below) for reading a manuscript, offering suggestions, and writing blurbs
- To the Mississippi Conference of the United Methodist Church, its bishop (Hope Morgan Ward mentioned above), District Superintendent Willis Britt, the rest of the cabinet, and my colleagues in ordained ministry
- To the Course of Study in Israel faculty and students
- To the Mississippi Course of Study School faculty and students
- To Charles Page and the friends and faculty of the Jerusalem Institute for Biblical Exploration
- To David Upshaw, Rod Dumas, Robert Lucas, and everyone at Perichoresis Ministry (and its director, Baxter Kruger, mentioned above)
- To Don Patterson, Geoffrey Joyner, Joe Landrum, Gene Martino, Sessions Polk, and the rest of the Brothers of the Bread
- To Newton, Maben, and Magee United Methodist Churches
- To "Bert's Class" at Galloway United Methodist Church, Jackson, Mississippi

- To Reita Keyes, Karl Holcomb, Hazel Cunningham, Donna Davis, and the folks at Flora United Methodist Church who attended classes on the book
- To Ann May, Dot Manor, Earl Boyd, Marie Lungrin, Beverly Willis, the late James Willis, and the rest at the Bentonia United Methodist Church
- To Marvin United Methodist Church in Florence, Mississippi
- To my teachers: Ed Friedman, Fred Craddock, Robert Capon, Ken Bailey, Jerome Murphy-O'Connor, Bargil Pixner, Leen Ritmeyer, and Joe Zias
- To Mrs. Carlyn Friedman
- To famous people who have inspired me: Michelangelo Buonarroti, Winston Churchill, Wolfgang Amadeus Mozart, Frank Zappa, Arturo Sandoval, William Shakespeare, Earnest Hemingway, John Wesley
- To supportive friends who risked believing in me: Butch and Judy McCall, Marc and Ina Magee, Ken Gilburth, Sam Morris, Bob Kohler, Rex Matthews, Bob Hermetz, and Hank Knight
- To my grandmother, Susan Segers (better known to her grandchildren as Minkie), who taught me English grammar one Saturday morning
- To my parents, brothers, and sister: Bob and Janet Gary, Mike Gary and family, Bill Gary and family, and Susan Gary Ashe and family
- To my children and grandchildren: Martha, Will, and Anna Gary; Paul, Rebecca, and Sam Sims; Chris, Cory, and Taylor Peusch; and Mac McKnight
- To my wife, Kathy.

INTRODUCTION

You must have noticed that we Christians tend to set great store by acting respectable, looking nice, and being presentable. I do not know anyone who would argue with that observation. I do not know many who see anything wrong with being respectable, nice, and presentable either. Clergy and laypersons alike. This goes for Christians regardless of which church you attend, or how often, if at all. The tendency to maintain the status quo is so commanding today that, if something does not seem respectable, nice, or presentable, it will almost certainly be viewed suspiciously in Christian circles, and even possibly regarded as un-Christian.

You might as well take your own pulse on this issue, right now, as you begin reading this book: In your heart, do you tend to see everything respectable, nice, and presentable as Christian? And to be Christian must you strive to be respectable, nice, and presentable?

Though it seems improbable, even impossible, we Christians may be too often guilty of reducing Christianity to mere social etiquette. Being well dressed and well behaved seem to have taken their place among the central tenets of Christianity. Yet Jesus himself said, "Woe to you, teachers of the law and Pharisees, you hypocrites! You clean the outside of the cup and dish, but inside they are full of greed and self-indulgence. Blind Pharisee! First clean the inside of the cup and dish, and then the outside also will be clean" (Mt 23:25–26, NIV).

I am concerned that we Christians are—and have been for some time—acting and talking too much like the very leaders in Jerusalem that Jesus condemned. For his opponents, appearance and propriety were first and foremost. Hunger for community recognition and visibility consumed them. Read Matthew 23, and then take an honest look at churches today.

If a plan does not enhance prestige and standing—*in the community and in comparison to "competing" churches*—then does it get sufficient support? Are we Christians guilty of the very thing Jesus hated, the very thing he attacked relentlessly: religious hypocrisy?

"Hypocrisy." Its origin is the Greek word *hupokrisis* (ὑπόκρισις). Translated literally, it means *under judgment* or *under division*. Compare the word "hypo-dermic," which means *under skin*. In its everyday usage in the time of Jesus, the term hypocrite referred to a dramatist, a theatrical actor, a thespian, a performer, or one who portrayed a character in a play. Hypocrisy was to act a part on stage.

So when Jesus called someone a hypocrite, he was calling him an actor. The meaning carries over to modern English, where a hypocrite is one who pretends to believe or feel a certain way, or who feigns virtue and character where none exists. So hypo-crisy assumes a divided nature, the real and the mask. To speak with a forked tongue, to be double-minded, to be two-faced, or to be double-dealing are all good imagery for hypocrisy. The inside and the outside do not match. Jesus quoted Isaiah saying, "This people honors me with their lips, but their hearts are far from me" (Mt 15:8, NIV).

Here are the questions that run to the heart of the matter. Where in Scripture does Jesus put a premium on acting respectable, nice, and presentable? In Matthew, Mark, Luke, or John—the four New Testament Gospels—in what chapter does etiquette get first billing? In which Gospel does Jesus instruct us to pay special attention to being well dressed and well behaved, to appearance and propriety, to visibility and recognition, or to prestige and standing?

If someone could only find these verses in the Scriptures, they could write a book about it, giving all of us biblical instructions on how to be well groomed, socially acceptable, and highly esteemed. If that is what Jesus said, we could certainly use a book on it. It might be entitled: *Looking Good for Jesus.*

Or: *Why Everyone Liked Jesus, and How You Can Be Liked Too.*
Or: *Christian Recognition—The Art of Getting the Accolades You
Deserve.* Sarcasm aside, these fictitious titles tragically express
the overriding priorities among many of today's Christians—
laypersons and clergy. Who can argue that we churchgoers,
individually and collectively, place priority on looking good,
being liked, and getting recognized? Not coincidentally, Jesus
rejected these priorities with word and deed. That is precisely
what this book will fully expose.

I will address Christian hypocrisy by going back to original passages in the Gospels that reveal not a cautious, image-
conscious Jesus, but a provocative, politically incorrect cage-
rattler for whom appearance and reputation meant nothing.
Our look at the Gospels should reveal not a people-pleasing
Jesus, but a "raw nerve" Jesus, one who—by present standards
of "Christian" social etiquette—acts in very un-Christian
ways!

Jesus deserves to be seen and heard, even if what he says
and does clashes with one's previous images and assumptions.
Specifically, we will look at those times when Jesus said a
big, flat-out No to requests, advice, or instructions. We will
look at those times when Jesus checked out (got up and left),
no matter what anyone else said or thought. We will look at
those times when Jesus created disturbances very much on
purpose. We will examine specific teachings that are not nice
in the least, and were never meant to be. And we will expose
what was extreme and offensive about Jesus's death, and what
was scandalous about Christianity's first sermons. Finally, *Jesus
Unplugged* concludes with an epilogue for the contemporary
church and its leaders.

At the end of each chapter you will find an *Unplug Your
Mind* question. These "wrap up" questions are not necessarily
the key questions, meaning they are neither the only questions nor the most important ones. But I doubt that you will
find them either irrelevant or boring. Use them as discussion
starters.

Also here and there you will see a bracketed **FYI**. This stands for "For Your Information." These contain related biblical or historical or archaeological details. I think of them as little whitewater rapids of further study. They take you on a detour, if detours are something you want to take. But you can skip them if you like and stay in the central flow of the book.

This book is meant to be inspiring, though not in the popular sense of the word. This is no daily devotional guide. If reading this book turns out to be anything like the experience of writing it, it might even be *disturbing*. And, in a sense, that is the book's intent. Perhaps it will be for you an inspirational disturbance. Or a disturbing inspiration! For better or for worse. To accomplish this, we will go to provocative passages in the Gospels, passages that have been avoided or sanitized over the years by pastors, teachers, and Christian writers.

Fans of MTV should enjoy my dubbing of these teachings *Jesus Unplugged*, a reference to the program where artists play in a small, up-close-and-personal venue, minus the massive amplification and cavernous arenas usually associated with rock concerts. It is mesmerizing to have the distance between the artist and the audience removed. There they are, musician and fans, face to face. For the artist there is nowhere to hide, putting his creativity and passion on the line, live with cameras rolling, no second takes. That is what is meant by *Jesus Unplugged*: live-and-in-person, up-close-and-personal, face-to-face, absorbing the words and actions of Jesus at his raw and provocative best.

Mel Gibson's movie, *The Passion*, portrayed how much the religious leaders of Jesus's day *hated* Jesus. Though Mr. Gibson's film is scripturally wrong on many points, in this he is 100 percent correct: Jesus *was* hated by the Judean authorities. *Jesus Unplugged*, however, takes you to the original Gospels themselves, and in plain words shows you what Mr. Gibson's movie did not: *why* they hated him. The Bible is extremely open and frank about this. It introduces us to a Jesus who is loved and hated, and it explains the reasons for these extreme responses. To come close and meet this loved and hated Jesus, turn the page.

1

HE SAID NO TO ACQUAINTANCES

"Let what you say be simply 'Yes' or 'No.'"
—Matthew 5:37a

With all the requests Jesus had to heal, and with all the demands placed on him, it only stands to reason that he would say No once in a while. But Jesus said No quite often—so often that it is startling. Though perhaps we should not be surprised. Someone with a strong character would by necessity need to be able to say Yes and No and mean both. Jesus himself said, "Let what you say be simply Yes or No; anything more than this comes from evil" (Mt 5:37, ESV).

Nevertheless, hearing Jesus say No, if not a surprise, is still a problem. It is perhaps the one word Christians do not want him to say. Maybe that is the reason that this business of Jesus saying No might be resisted, even denied. At the very least it is uncomfortable for believers to consider. Certainly no one who loves Jesus wants to hear his Nos. Yet to be true to the gospels, each and every No that Jesus spoke must be heard, just as faithfully as we have listened to his Yeses. His Nos had unexpected wisdom. But see and hear for yourself.

Jesus Refuses to Help Two Brothers
Settle an Inheritance Battle

A man in the crowd demanded, "Teacher, tell my brother to divide the family inheritance with me." Jesus refused, saying, "Friend, who set me as a judge or arbitrator over you?" (Lk 12:13–21, NRSV).

Rather than settle the estate case, suddenly Jesus launched into a parable:

> "There was a rich man whose land produced a bountiful harvest. He asked himself, 'What shall I do, for I do not have space to store my harvest?' And he said, 'This is what I shall do: I shall tear down my barns and build larger ones. There I shall store all my grain and other goods and I shall say to myself, "Now as for you, you have so many good things stored up for many years, rest, eat, drink, be merry!" But God said to him, 'You fool, this night your life will be demanded of you; and the things you have prepared, to whom will they belong?'" (Lk 12:16–20, NAB).

Having full barns does not make you rich toward God, Jesus concluded.

This is an appropriate parable, an important parable, full of irony and humor. But did it solve the problem? The brothers still did not have a ruling about the inheritance. One could argue that Jesus fixed nothing.

Christians who go charging in to fix the personal problems of others should be taking notes. Jesus refused to get involved in this private family matter, deciding instead to use the opportunity to teach. So why not step in? Why not insist that the brothers divide the inheritance fairly so that both parties are satisfied? Why not get involved, fix the problem? Would that not be the "Christian" thing to do?

While we cannot know why exactly, we do know that Jesus immediately told a parable cartooning the ridiculousness and danger of greed. Jesus was unwilling to finalize the breach that greed had created between these brothers. This inheritance issue had driven them further apart, and if Jesus had ruled on the matter finally, the destruction of their relationship might have been complete.

no heart
reply
to h altar?

So Jesus was likely more concerned about brothers remaining brothers than what was fair financially. He refused to
take sides. He refused to make a ruling or give advice. Actually,
he refused to get involved at all, except that he told everyone
a parable about how greed is futile and it leads to isolation.
Obviously, Jesus risked disappointing the brothers in saying
No. But more was at stake than mere property.

In the end, it was all up to the brothers themselves. Did
they have ears with which to hear the parable Jesus told or
not? Luke does not tell us how it turned out for them. He
leaves us hoping the brothers found reconciliation.

Can believers stomach the thought that Jesus sometimes
refuses to fix things in their lives, leaving them to struggle
and suffer? If so, what does this say about God? One way to
put it is that *God does not over-function in people's lives.*[1] To over-
function is to lose the sense of a boundary between self and
other, allowing oneself to become over-invested and over-involved. What great favor would God be doing by forgetting
the gift of human freedom he gave us, opting for a new heavy-
handed approach? What if God stopped inviting and started
coercing? Would we really prefer having no freedom and no
choice? Granted, freedom of choice means we struggle an
awful lot about what to do, what to say, and which way to go.
But would it really be better to have freedom removed just to
avoid the struggles we inherit with the gift of choice?

Strangely enough, the old theodicy argument is being addressed in the story of these two brothers and their inheritance.
[**FYI:** Theodicy is the discussion of why there is suffering if
God is all good and powerful.] The brothers seemed willing
to forgo their freedom to get this painful inheritance problem
fixed. They were ready to allow a third party to decide for
them in an attempt to end their suffering (or feed their greed).
But that third party—Jesus—would not take their freedom or
their suffering away! He refused to steal their right to decide,
allowing them to continue hurting. Jesus chose not to rob

not mystical.

them of their right to work things out, concerning both the inheritance and, more importantly, their relationship as brothers. He placed the choice and the struggle right back in their laps. Jesus seemed to value the difficulty of freedom more than they did. He also rejected the quick fix. This is divine behavior. God, in terms of theodicy, rejects quick fixes and affirms the struggle inherent in freedom of choice.

There is also the issue of dependency. Look at how Jesus refused to allow the brothers to *depend* on him to make the decision for them. For his part, Jesus votes for them making an *in*-dependent decision. He did not see himself as needed, and he would not participate in that way. It was not that he did not care about them as persons, or that he did not care that they were struggling, because I believe that he did. But Jesus's expression of care came in the form of limit-setting on *himself!* Maybe you have heard of the concept from Jewish mysticism (more recently known as Kabbalah) called Zimzum (or Tsimtsum). It refers to the idea that in creation God shrank back, creating space for creation. Similarly, Jesus refused to "invade" the brothers' space. Self-restraint a divine attribute? The word No an expression of care? Without a doubt.

Additionally, Jesus used humor to combat seriousness. The weight of the brothers' problem is palpable in the narrative. They are stuck. They are ready to go to court, and in fact are asking the rabbi from Nazareth to render a ruling on their case. But Jesus, after asking them, *Who made me the judge?*—a question leaning toward humor in and of itself—then follows with a silly cartoon-of-a-parable, one clearly intended to be humorous. He presses greed to its illogical and absurd conclusion: Here is an isolated scrooge, talking to himself, and hoarding stuff he does not need and never will. *Humor is the only antidote to seriousness.*[2] And stuck people get very serious, as do stuck businesses, stuck churches, and especially stuck families.

Once there was a woman whose husband embarrassed her terribly by falling asleep in front of guests. The man would drift off and snore whenever they had company, right there in the living room. She was too afraid to entertain, and she could not stand the isolation this had created. But she could not risk inviting friends for dinner, for the bear might slip into hibernation at any moment! Her rabbi's advice? "Invite your guests, and the second you sense your husband getting droopy, say to them, 'I can see that my husband is falling asleep. Let's go in the other room for coffee so that we won't disturb him.' Then get up and serve your guests coffee in the other room. Don't even concern yourself with embarrassing him. He can handle it. And, by the way, has he shown concern or remorse for the embarrassment he has caused you?" So, the woman reluctantly did as the rabbi advised. She saw her husband getting ready to doze in the living room after dinner. She said to her guests, "Obviously my husband likes to sleep after his meals. Let's have our coffee on the porch so we don't disturb him." And she walked to the porch where a fresh pot had already brewed and where cups, spoons, sugar, and cream awaited the dinner guests. She held a cup, poured, and turned to offer it to someone when she notice her husband standing in the doorway, eyes wide and unblinking. He never fell asleep in front of company again.[3]

Playfulness works. When a family is stuck and serious, there are precious few cures. Sometimes, however, humor can break the spell. Jesus's comic parable may very well have been intended to do just that. But did it work? Did the brothers snap out of it the way the drowsy husband did?

Unfortunately, what the brothers chose to do remains a mystery. Did they reconcile, or did they just go to another rabbi for a ruling? We will never know. Yet the important thing in this story is not what finally happened. The point Jesus made by word and deed is that the choice concerning the inheritance was theirs. Jesus said No, it's not my problem.

God does not over-function. Jesus does not over-function. Then why are "caring" Christians, then, so inclined to over-function?

Unplug Your Mind: Why are "caring" Christians so inclined to become over-anxious and over-invested and over-involved in other people's lives?

Jesus Refuses to Let the Man Leave with Him

Woody Allen could have written this scene (Mk 5:1–20). Jesus sailed over to the Gentile side (the east side) of the Sea of Galilee ... on purpose. He went ashore at a cemetery ... God only knows why. Nearby, there was a herd of swine ... saints preserve us.

Gentiles, corpses, and pigs, oh my! [**FYI:** All three are sources of ritual defilement under Jewish laws of purity. Any one of them could render one unclean, a state that Jews avoided in order not to break the laws outlined in the Hebrew Bible. The presence of all three at the same time is dramatic from a Jewish point of view.]

Defilement was imminent, and Jesus's sanity must have been questioned by the disciples, as it was on many occasions. But there's more. To top it off, an uncircumcised maniac came howling out of one of the burial caves, broken chains dangling from his wrists. He was running straight for them, chains rattling, bare feet pounding, dust flying, screaming over and over at the top of his lungs, "Jesus, don't torture me! Jesus, don't torture me!" Horror writer Stephen King would love this!

Jesus, demonstrating impossible calm, saw this as an opportunity to initiate a pleasant conversation with the jolly fellow, while undoubtedly the disciples went into seizures. Jesus simply asked the man his name. The lunatic said, "My name is Legion, for we are many." [**FYI:** A unit of Roman soldiers numbering about 5,000 men was called a legion. The man was telling Jesus that an army of demons resided in him.] Legion begged Jesus not to send the demons out of the country, but instead into the nearby herd of swine. Jesus must have found this humorous. The unclean spirits want to go into the unclean swine? *Serves them right!* So Jesus permitted them to go into the swine, but when the demons went into the swine, the swine rushed into the Sea of Galilee and drowned. Another layer of humor! Evil spirits in that day were believed to have come from beneath the sea. That is why sailors and fishermen were considered to be brave and half crazy, for to drown at sea meant dying at the mercy of the origin of evil.

To recap, Jesus and his followers sail to the unclean Gentile shore of the Sea of Galilee and come ashore at an unclean cemetery, from which an unclean Gentile lunatic full of unclean demons accosts them. Jesus sends the unclean spirits into the unclean pigs who run into the sea to drown in its unclean depths. It is hard to retell this story and "keep it clean!"

Soon the exorcised madman was clothed and in his right mind. The swineherders saw all of this and ran to town to report it. The townsfolk came running to see what was going on, and they did not like what they saw. Rather than celebrating their kinsman's good fortune, they panicked and evicted Jesus on the spot! As Jesus was unwilling to stay where he is not wanted (and still is today), he stepped back into the boat. As he did so, the ex-nutcase asked Jesus if he might be allowed to go with him: *Please, I beg of you, let me come with you!* (based on Mk 5:18).

Taking the man with them would have been the kind and the easy thing to do. The fellow wanted to follow Jesus, and he could have provided an excellent witness for what God can do, much as Mary of Magdala (Mary Magdalene) did. She too had demons cast out of her. [**FYI:** Contrary to popular belief and folklore, Mary Magdalene was not a harlot. At least the Bible never says so. All we know about Mary from Scripture is that she was from Magdala on the northwest shore of the Sea of Galilee, Jesus cast seven demons out of her, she helped fund Jesus's ministry (Lk 8:1–3), and she is the first disciple to whom the risen Lord appeared. (Jn 20:11–18) Mary Magdalene is not named as one of the women who washed Jesus's feet (Lk 7:38; Jn 12:3), and she is not named as the woman of Jerusalem caught in adultery (Jn 8:1–11).]

Did the town really want "Legion" around now? Were they celebrating his good fortune? Did they care a whit? The poor guy couldn't continue to live in the cemetery, could he? Where was he supposed to go? True, he was a Gentile, and as the follower of a Jewish rabbi there would be complications. Yet that must have seemed a minor problem to the man at the time. *Why not me?* he must have thought. But Jesus said No. The man was not allowed to go with him.

We're left with two questions: Why did the people want Jesus to leave? And why did Jesus refuse the man's request and order him to stay?

Why did the townspeople ask Jesus to leave? Some commentaries say the people were angry about the pigs. There was a lot of lost revenue when those porkers drowned. But that cannot be the reason. They asked Jesus to leave not when they saw that the pigs had died, but when they saw that the town nutcase was suddenly sane. *That* is what disturbed them.

Change disturbs systems. The "crazy man" was what might be called, in psychological circles, their "identified child." In plain English, they could scapegoat him and go on believing blissfully that *he* was the problem. Especially as long as he was living in the cemetery draped in chains. The townsfolk would never have to examine their own insanity as long as they had a designated lunatic around!

We liked you better the way you were before. And in some families or communities, healing or maturation create a disturbance. The system reacts to correct itself. Those who change are pressured in subtle and not-so-subtle ways to go back to the way they were. Since our friend could not go back to being naked and wacky and sleeping in a sarcophagus, what was he supposed to do? The terms for his being "one of them" were that he stayed naked and whacky and sleeping in a coffin. That was the deal, take it or leave it. Jesus messed up everything! Things were fine before *he* showed up. He should have realized before he stuck his nose into their business that every town needs a prodigal to gossip about, just like every family needs a black sheep to blame.

But why did Jesus order the man to stay? More specifically, why did he order the man to go into town to tell his "friends" about what God did to change his life? Well, apparently this is the way human institutions (families, towns, corporations, countries) change, or at least start to get unstuck. It begins with leadership. Someone speaks and acts in a differentiated way. Someone innovates.[4] Someone sees the big picture and exposes it. That is the way it works. Yet the "system" will usually resist the truth, reject the innovation, and stop the change *if it can*. That was the great challenge before this poor man from Gergesa. Because sometimes if you don't like the message, you simply kill the messenger. Jesus issued his marching orders: *Move back into your hometown and tell your story to everybody.*

Did the man once named Legion succeed in reentering the town on new terms, as a sane man? Did he, therefore, cause the town to face its own demons? We do not know the answers to these questions. All that the Scriptures say is that they were amazed. But we are all familiar with the situation, and the dilemma is closer to us than we comfortably imagine.

Family systems therapist Rabbi Edwin Friedman claimed to spend only 10 percent of his time helping people to change. People who came to him usually wanted to change, or had *already* changed. Yet he spent 90 percent—*90 percent!*—of his time doing something else. Guess what it was? Ninety percent of his time in counseling was spent helping those who had changed to deal with the reactivity of their families—and other systems—pressuring them to go back to the way they were! Ninety percent of his counseling consisted of coaching folks to hang in there in spite of pressure from those who liked them better when they were crazy, sick, drunk, or depressed!

Could Jesus have known that hope for healing in Gergesa was for this ex-lunatic to go home as a constant reminder that he was no longer an available fall guy? Was Jesus's purpose in sending him back to stop the townsfolk from projecting their psychosis onto him? Perhaps we need for Jesus to have twenty-first century psychological training to answer this question in the affirmative. Still, to rephrase the question, could Jesus have known that it was important for these people to face their former nutcase, and thus face themselves? It's possible.

Interestingly, a suggested psychological technique for healing and change goes right along with what Jesus ordered this man to do. *If you want to learn how to be nonreactive at work, go to your mother's house and say something to make her anxious!*[5] The idea of this is that if a grown daughter can learn to be nonreactive in her panicked mother's presence, then she can do it anywhere! Could it be that the completion of the crazy man's healing would be for him to be sane *in* the town, not just outside of it? It is one thing to be a mature, healthy adult on neutral turf. It's another thing all together to do it in Mom and Dad's living room.

No, Jesus said. *Go home and keep telling Gergesa what God has done for you.* A fitting punishment for a cruel town? Or perhaps it is the completion of a miraculous transformation for one villager and medicine for a sick village.

Unplug Your Mind: Why does your family have the power to trigger anxiety in you like nothing else on earth?

Jesus Refuses Three Times to Help a Desperate Woman

If there is a more complex and disturbing story in the Gospels than the previous one, it would be this one. This example of Jesus saying No almost did not make the final cut for this book, not because it is the most disturbing of all Jesus's refusals, but because it is unclear why Jesus said No three times, and whether he really meant it. This is likely the scene that first comes to mind when one thinks of startling passages in the Gospels. It is the story of Jesus's encounter with a Syrophoenecian woman (Mt 15:21–28; Mk 7:24–30).

Jesus had checked out (withdrawn, left), something he did often; most of those occasions will be discussed specifically in Chapter 4. He was in danger and under considerable pressure in Galilee, so he went north to the region of Tyre and Sidon called Phoenicia, and stayed at an unspecified house where he made every effort to make sure that no one knew he was there. It is important at this time to note that Mark says Jesus tried to escape notice for reasons to be addressed later. But the effort failed when a Syrophoenician woman showed up, barged in, and crashed the party. Somehow his cover had been blown. She knew Jesus by reputation. Matthew says she came out and started shouting: *Help me, Lord! My daughter is tortured by a demon.* Demons again. But Matthew and Mark do not tell us this time whether it was insanity or some other ailment. (Demons were thought to be the cause of most psychological and physiological conditions.) We will never know what was wrong with this woman's daughter, but we can assume that it was serious enough to make her desperate.

Three times—count them—*Jesus refused to help her.*

First refusal: He did not answer her at all. He appeared to ignore her. But she did not stop. She just kept on shouting. The disciples began to get annoyed. They realized that this woman was not going to relent, so they told Jesus to send her away. You have to feel for Jesus's predicament. He was seeking anonymity and did not find it, seeking quiet that this woman disrupted, and then the disciples began telling him what to do, which, as you will see, they did quite often!

Second refusal: Ignoring her did not work. But Jesus seemed reluctant to dismiss her without explanation. So he said, "I was sent only to the lost sheep of the house of Israel" (Mt 15:24, NRSV). His refusal to help her appears to be on the grounds that she was not a Jew. The scene conjures images of "whites only" water fountains. Our sensibilities toward an inclusive Gospel can hardly accept these words, even though two Gospels record them. Luke, perhaps showing superior judgment, omits this scene entirely! Maybe Jesus, at least at that point in his ministry, really saw his mission as exclusive to Jews. Look at the context: At that moment he was not in Galilee or Judea where Jews lived. Therefore, he must have considered himself to be off duty. This was private time. He was secretly residing on foreign soil. He did not want his cover blown, nor did he wish to "work." Perhaps he felt no obligation to help a foreigner, and he refused her a second time.

Third refusal: But she would not be denied. Boldly, she came forward to kneel at Jesus's feet, begging, "Lord, help me." But Jesus seems to have had no intention of helping her. His reply sounded harsh, even cold. "It is not fair to take the children's food and throw it to the dogs" (Mt 15:26, NRSV). Essentially, Jesus called her a dog, which of course is an epithet Jews often used to refer to Gentiles. This statement is antithetical to any image of Jesus that we cherish. It borders on cruel.

Thankfully, the story ends well. The woman did not take offense at being called a dog. Instead, she took the metaphor and ran with it in hopes, we assume, of changing Jesus's mind. She said, "Yes, Lord, yet even the dogs eat the crumbs that fall from the master's table" (Mt 15:27, NRSV). She just would not give up. Three refusals from the master, and she was at his feet, hanging in there. This last statement of hers seems to have done the trick. In Mark, he praised what she said. In Matthew, Jesus praised her great faith. At that point, he sent her on her way with the assurance that her daughter had been healed.

It is hard to say what is going on in the story of the Syrophoenician woman. What Jesus was thinking is not apparent to us. All we have are ancient Scriptures, none of which are psychologically analytical. Anyone claiming to know the mind of Jesus, his inner thoughts and motives, is delusional. Yet there has to be a reason for his seeming callousness to this desperate woman's pleas.

Writers have abundant theories that are as close as a library or bookstore, or your next web search on Google. Many of them claim Jesus was testing her faith. There are many theories trying to explain—or *explain away*—this difficult text. What can we infer that has not been covered before? Is there another angle on this?

What we can add or interpret is speculative at best, as are any and all attempts to explain why Jesus refused this poor woman repeatedly, and seemingly harshly. To conclude that he was not altogether serious in what he said to the woman will require us to imagine Jesus having a mischievous, playful sense of humor. Yet to hear Jesus's words as playful, as salty, as a bit tongue-in-cheek, changes the whole tone of the scene.

Counselors often have to deal with the very serious problem of suicidal counselees. One such counselor had a unique approach to this problem, and no one under his care ever committed suicide. To a woman talking about ending it all, he once remarked that if he had the problems she had, he would probably kill himself too. To a man having suicidal thoughts, he made suggestions on the best methods, and the pros and cons of each. It seems cruel and cold. But the end result was worth the risk of sounding callous. Both counselees laughed during their counseling sessions, and their mental health improved from that point forward.

To reread Jesus's words in the context of this "absurd" advice for suicidal counselees points to the possibility that Jesus may not have been entirely serious. Could it be that he was being straight-faced but facetious, and that *she knew it* and played along? She was, after all, a woman of ancient Canaanite blood, a bold and courageous woman who did what few among her kind would have done in approaching a Jewish teacher, presuming to ask for his assistance. This is a gutsy move, and Jesus certainly must have taken note of that. Perhaps he was impressed from the start with the foreign woman's spirit. Perhaps she sensed that while the disciples were quite seriously irritated with her, their master was *not*, so she continued to plead.

Cultural analysis of this story supports this view. "Challenge and riposte" was a favorite strategy of winning debates in Jesus's culture, and Jesus was a master at it. For example, the Pharisees once challenged Jesus about his disciples not washing their hands ritually. [**FYI:** It was a Jewish tradition to wash to the wrists or elbows before eating (The Greek word πυγμή translates literally "with a/the fist," and the meaning is unclear).] " ... for the Pharisees, and all the Jews, if they do not wash the hands to the wrist, do not eat, holding the tradition of the elders ... " (Mk 7:3, Young's Literal Translation).

Jesus began his riposte with an insult: *You hypocrites! It is not what goes into your mouth that defiles you, but what comes out!* Jesus responds to challenges almost the same way every time: Insult and riposte. And no one *ever* bests him at this ... except this one little foreign woman of Syrophoenecia! In this exchange, it is *she* who out-ripostes Jesus.

Culturally, it is she who comes out on top, according to anthropologist John Pilch:

> "[Jesus] acknowledges the woman's skill at riposte ("for saying that") and declares the favor granted. In Matthew's version, Jesus's final comment ("let it be done for you as you wish" 15:28) is the Middle Eastern way of *giving up* in an argument one doesn't expect to win. The woman has proven a worthy match and bested Jesus." (italics mine)[6]

Perhaps it was a test of wits to Jesus and the woman, a playful war of words. Perhaps it was an argument that Jesus did not mind losing, and that he had no intention of winning, one that compassion compelled him to lose. Reread it. Try seeing the conversation between Jesus and this crafty, persistent woman as a saucy repartee, and the whole scene changes.

Now consider this: It is the disciples once again who are not "getting it." Jesus had set it up so that they would hear from this woman's own mouth what Jesus has been trying to demonstrate all along. Yes, the "party line" in Jewish circles concerning Gentiles was that they were dogs, that they were not included in the "heavenly banquet," and that the Messiah was not sent to or for them. And Jesus tows this party line facetiously, setting up the woman's opportunity to deliver the zinger, *the Gospel itself*, that God's Son has come for *the world*, Gentiles too. *Even the dogs eat the crumbs that fall from the master's table.*

The disciples should have understood this before the encounter with this woman. Jesus healed a Roman centurion's servant. He was no Jew (Mt 8:5–13). He healed a possessed Gentile known as Legion (Mk 5:1–20). He reached out to a Samaritan woman and her whole village (Jn 4:1–42). He healed the son of Herod's royal official (Jn 4:46-54). He preached to Nazareth about how Elijah and Elisha were sent to foreigners instead of Israel, a sermon for which he was almost stoned (Lk 4:16-30). A Gentile woman named Joanna may have even helped to finance his ministry. (Lk 8:3) [**FYI:** Although Joanna is a Jewish name, she was married to Herod Antipas's steward, a Roman named Chuza, so her origins are uncertain. How a woman in the court of Antipas, the wife of a valued court official, was able to travel with a Jewish rabbi, even going to Jerusalem and witnessing his crucifixion and resurrection (Mk 15:40–41; Lk 24:10) without getting caught also remains uncertain. Either she was able to keep the purpose of her travel and spending from her husband, or her husband knew what she was doing and protected her secret. Jesus was wanted by Herod (Lk 13:31); we will never know how Joanna was able to conceal her loyalty and aid to a fugitive Jewish rabbi.]

The point? A Gentile ministry was in Jesus's plan *all along*. It was already underway. But it was the disciples, famous especially in Mark's Gospel for their cluelessness, who need the lesson repeated again and again. What better way to reinforce the lesson than to hear it from the lips of the Syrophoenecian woman herself? Jesus helped the foreign woman teach the Gospel to his own disciples!

Now perhaps it is clear why this story almost did not make the cut for this book. The temptation to "fix" the story, to explain the harsh words and rejections, is reason enough to avoid it. But it is not the purpose of this book to fix, sanitize, or censor Jesus in any way. Quite the opposite. So what makes this story an unusual entry in this book is that Jesus's three refusals in this particular case may not have been seriously intended. Admittedly, he could have been dead serious. Yet, if so, we are faced with a flawed Christ—a Christ who is prejudiced, exclusive, and lacking in compassion.

Tongue-in-cheek or dead serious? Are we to see Jesus as capable of teasing repartee with a gutsy woman, or guilty of callousness toward a desperate woman? Take your pick. I choose the former. Either way, this scene forces us to readjust our image of him. And that serves the purpose.

Unplug Your Mind: Can you hear your own voice hurling facetious insults and epithets, or are you too straightlaced to act like Jesus?

Jesus Refuses Advice from Friendly Pharisees

Jesus had some acquaintances among the Pharisees who supported him and, it appears, looked out for him. They came to him as he was heading for Jerusalem. They were concerned that he had returned to Judea. *Get out of here*, they said. *Herod is planning to kill you* (based on Lk 13:31). It is nice to have friends looking out for you, especially friends in high places. These Pharisees gathered vital intelligence for Jesus, and they delivered it promptly. Further, they advised Jesus that he should leave before he was caught. Every leader needs intel and security and counsel.

What is revealing, however, is Jesus's response. Clearly, he has made up his mind to go to Jerusalem (Lk 9:51); it was his destiny. He had predicted his death (Mk 8:31), and was going under protest from Peter and the others. He suddenly strode ahead of them so that they were amazed and afraid (Mk 10:32). This was the backdrop when the Pharisees warned Jesus to retreat. Predictably, Jesus's response was *No. I'm not turning back.*

This time Jesus said more than No. He not only refused to leave, but he challenged that bully King Herod and used an insulting epithet to do so!

You go tell that fox (a Jew turned Roman; a traitor)
if he wants an appointment with me, he'll have to wait.
Tell him I'm tied up today. I have a 1 p.m. exorcism, and
a 4 p.m. healing. And I'm booked up solid tomorrow too.
But I might be able to squeeze him in the next day, as
I have an important appointment in Jerusalem anyway.
Tell him he can find me there, because God forbid a
prophet should be murdered outside Jerusalem. Go on.
Go tell him now! (based on Lk 13:32–33)

There it is again: The surprising boldness. The sharp humor. The wit. Jesus was a force to be reckoned with now
that he had made up his mind. He was going to Jerusalem to
challenge the temple leadership come hell or high water. His
destiny drove him. They literally would have to kill him to
stop him now. Run away? Hide? Back down? Leave? No, No,
a thousand times No. Retreat was not an option.

Unplug Your Mind: When was the last time you stood up to
a bully?

Jesus Refuses Advice from Friendly Pharisees Again

Jesus entered the city limits of Jerusalem at Bethpage riding a
donkey (Mt 21:1–9; Mk 11:1–10; Lk 19:29–38; Jn 12:12–15),
a blatantly messianic thing to do. "Rejoice greatly, O daughter Zion! Shout aloud, O daughter Jerusalem! Lo, your king
comes to you; triumphant and victorious is he, humble and
riding on a donkey, on a colt, the foal of a donkey." (Zec 9:9,
NRSV).

Things got a little out of hand. Crowds of people waived
palm branches, Israel's symbol of national identity and independence. They shouted Hosanna, by which they most
probably meant *Save us, we pray!* Save us from what? Save us
presumably from the Romans. They sang or chanted: *Blessed*

is the king! Blessed is the king who comes in the name of the Lord! Blessed is the coming kingdom of our ancestor David! (based on Mt 21:9; Mk 11:9-10; Lk 19:38; Jn 12:13)

Whatever their intent, the crowd was roaring as it came down the Mount of Olives toward the temple, people shouting a lot of presumptuous claims about Jesus. It was a loud, conspicuous scene by all accounts.

Some Pharisees in the crowd were concerned: *Rabbi, make your disciples shut up!* they demanded (based on Lk 19:39). Friends or foes of Jesus could have said this. Probably they were friends since they were *in* the crowd, they expressed concern, and they offered sound advice. They did not want their colleague from Nazareth to get in trouble before he ever had a chance to explain himself at the temple. It was beginning to look and sound like a circus maximus! Managing the noise and hullabaloo seemed prudent to Jesus's allies among the Pharisees. They were probably thinking, *We're with you Jesus, but tone it down, for God's sake, before this gets completely unmanageable.*

Jesus's response?

I'm telling you, if I made them stop, the rocks would roar! (based on Lk 19:40).

Here is clear refusal to take sound political advice. *No,* he was saying. *There is no way I'm going to squelch this. This is my hour. This is their hour. Nothing will stop it now. Nothing.*

Unplug Your Mind: Have you ever experienced a wonderful celebration that took on a life of its own?

Conclusion

Brothers were desperate to get a legal ruling on their inheritance, and to these nameless acquaintances Jesus said No. A gentile healed of insanity wanted to leave his home and travel with Jesus, and to this nameless acquaintance Jesus said No. A foreign woman was desperate to get healing for her daughter, and to this nameless acquaintance Jesus said No three times (before giving in).

Nameless Pharisees warned Jesus to get out of Judea before Herod caught him and killed him, and to these nameless acquaintances Jesus said No. And Pharisees advised Jesus to tone down the parade of palms, and to these nameless acquaintances Jesus said No.

Whether a person wanted something or tried to help, Jesus retained the right to refuse them. But it was not only acquaintances he refused. He also refused disciples and opponents alike. That is the subject of the next chapter.

2

HE SAID NO
TO FOLLOWERS AND FOES ALIKE

"Beware when all speak well of you."

—Luke 6:26

I f you are one of those people who has a hard time saying No, you might well be shocked at the ease and frequency with which Jesus refused people. Most of us feel at least a little conflicted, especially when we are asked to chair the Parent Teacher Organization or direct next summer's Vacation Bible School. "No, thank you" is what you want to say, but what will people think? What will the principal think? What will the pastor think?

A lot of people struggle with saying No. But what about Jesus? Did he hesitate? Did he worry what people would think? Did he consider his reputation? Was he concerned with public opinion?

In the previous chapter as in this one, whether you are demanding, begging, or advising, whether you are friend, follower, or foe, the man from Nazareth of Galilee might very well say No.

Jesus Rejects His Disciples' Reasonable Plan

Maybe you are starting to see a pattern. Jesus was trying to get himself and the disciples away from the crowds. They were pressing him so much—without a break even to eat—that he had to make a decision. Jesus said, "Come with me by yourselves to a quiet place and get some rest" (Mk 6:31, NIV).

So they got into a boat to escape for some solitude. But the crowds followed them on foot along the shore, and Jesus, after some thought, decided to postpone their vacation. He went ashore and continued to minister, and the evening culminated with Jesus's feeding 5,000 men *plus* women and children with five loaves and two fish: one of his most familiar and favorite miracles, and one of the few events recorded in all four Gospels (Mt 14:13–21; Mk 6:30–44; Lk 9:10–17; Jn 6:1–15).

Jesus directed the disciples to have all the people sit down in groups on the grass. He took the five loaves and two fish and, looking up to heaven, gave thanks and broke the loaves. Then he gave them to his disciples to pass them out. Then he passed out the two fish. The large crowd ate and was satisfied, and the disciples picked up twelve basketfuls of broken pieces of bread and fish left over.

There will be more on the loaves and fishes event in Chapter 4. But one point needs to be made here. In this story, he says No to his *disciples.*

Let us back up. In this story, the story of the feeding of the five thousand (Mk 6:30–44), as it was getting late, the disciples apparently had a meeting where *they* decided what Jesus should do: He should send the people away to buy food for themselves. It was late. The people were hungry. The disciples took it upon themselves to come up with a reasonable solution. When they reported to Jesus what they had decided and told him what to do, guess what? He refused. He said, *No, you will give them food.*

Before we go rushing to the miracle, let us not fail to take note of his refusal. He said *I won't send them away.* Then he commanded the disciples to feed the crowd, a command that would have seemed highly unreasonable. *Be realistic, Jesus. It would take eight months' pay to feed that many people.* So much for their little board meeting. Farewell to rationality. They must have been thinking to themselves, *If only Jesus were more predictable, more cooperative, more controllable!*

So what was the problem? The problem was that Jesus was self-ish![1] Not selfish meaning only interested in himself. But self-ish, as in having a strong, clear, well defined, healthy sense of self. And having a strong sense of self means not being afraid to refuse the requests and demands made by those closest to him. The easy thing to do is go along with what others say, with what they want and direct. It does not seem to have bothered Jesus at all, however, to thwart their plan by refusing to play along. Of course, as it turned out, Jesus had other plans for how the disciples would feed the 5,000, but that will have to wait for now. So stay tuned for more.

First, we move to three consecutive refusals by Jesus to persons on the verge of discipleship (Lk 9:57–62) They are reversed here. That is, these three stories will be addressed in the opposite order that they occur in the Gospel of Luke.

Jesus set his face to go to Jerusalem and meet his fate (Lk 9:51), and on the way he encountered three would-be disciples with selfish agendas and excuses. To them Jesus said No in the harshest and most demanding terms.

Unplug Your Mind: When have you refused requests or demands made of you by colleagues or coworkers?

Jesus Rejects a Man's Proposal to Get Parental Permission

A would-be disciple wanted to "take leave" of his family before following Jesus to Jerusalem (Lk 9:61). Take leave does not mean say goodbye. It means ask permission.

"Mom? Dad? I met a traveling preacher today. I've never seen him before in my life. But he's going to Jerusalem to confront the establishment. We'll all probably get in a lot of trouble. I'd like to leave right now, and I'll probably never see you again. OK?"

"Why, sure, son," the Dad replies. "I see no problem with your abandoning your responsibilities to us and the family business. Why should honoring your father and mother keep you from launching out on a whim with a strange trouble-maker? Even if you never return, it will have been worth it for you to have the opportunity to neglect decency, responsibility, and obligation that you might satisfy your selfish impulse. Go ahead. You have our full blessing."

I hope you have not missed the sarcasm intended here. The sad truth of this story is how contemporary it is, and how similar this is to the situation adults face as they struggle to cut parental ties even today. Like many fledglings, this young man feels he must get his parent's permission to follow the impulse of life.

Yet Jesus said to the young man, "No one having put his hand on a plough, and looking back, is fit for the reign of God" (Lk 9:62, YLT). What he was saying was, *Those who do not cut the apron strings, those whose umbilical chords are still attached, are of no use to God's realm, period.*

How could Jesus have been any clearer? Jesus flat out refused the man's proposed condition of agreement: *No,* Jesus said, *you may not go ask permission. When following God, it cannot matter whether others approve or not, not even your parents. If you put your hand to the plow and keep looking back for approval, you will plow crooked, and we have no use for you. But if you can leave now, without parental approval, and not look back, that is a different story. Make your decision independent of your parents. Decide for yourself. You need no one's permission.*

Students of the Bible are often surprised that Jesus would take this position. Yet the Jesus of Scripture sometimes turns out to be very different from the sanitized version of Jesus dwelling in our churches and culture. Forget the delicate and dull Jesus some of us grew up with. Make way for a commanding, forceful Jesus.

Did the recruit leave without parental permission as Jesus wanted, or did he go back home? Luke does not say. His decision hangs in the air for us to ponder, along with our own.

Unplug Your Mind: How important is it to you to earn parental approval?

Jesus Rejects a Man's Proposal to Follow Him Later

This is one of the harshest-sounding statements Jesus is recorded to have said to any one person. *Let the dead bury their own dead.* "Jesus said to another, 'Follow me.' But he replied, 'Lord, first let me go and bury my father.' But Jesus said to him, 'Let the dead bury their own dead, but as for you, go and proclaim the kingdom of God'" (Lk 9:59–60, NEB).

This would-be disciple wanted to first bury his father, and then follow Jesus. Of course, most commentaries point out that the man's father is not dead. The young man's concern is that for a son to leave his father *before* his death is a serious community issue. There were strong cultural expectations, obligations, and regulations. The expectation was that a son did not leave his father, his father's home, and his father's business prior to his death. Even then, were he the oldest son, his responsibility to act as head of the household would be imposed. Most first-century Jewish communities would not have tolerated a son who abandons his father and his family (in other words, the parable of the prodigal son in Luke 15). This was unacceptable behavior—and punishable by stoning.

Jesus, nevertheless, told the poor fellow No. *Do not go back to your village, he said. They are all dead there. Let them bury themselves* (based on Lk 9:60).

These are harsh words. Jesus accused this prospective disciple's family and community of being dead—*spiritually* dead we presume. As difficult as it may be to fathom, and as painful as it is to consider, we are being asked to accept that people can be biologically alive but spiritually dead. What did he mean?

Again, we cannot be certain what Jesus was thinking. Yet, as in the previous story, a potential disciple of Jesus finds that the barrier to following him is not smoking, drinking, or gambling. Neither is it wine, women, and song. Nor is it drugs, pornography, or the occult. It is the grip his family and community had on him, their expectations and traditions. A powerful force even today. Family responsibilities make it very difficult to break away, either physically or emotionally. The question, *What of the traditions and expectations of where I was raised?* drowns out the sound of many a call from God. And that is how one becomes spiritually dead. That is how it is literally possible for the dead to bury the dead. It happens every day in a community near you!

No, Jesus said. *Forget the dead ways of the dead people in the dead town where you were raised. Come with me and proclaim life, the gospel, the kingdom.*

Forget a pale, pastel Jesus. Dismiss the retiring, faint-hearted Messiah. He was actually blunt and forcible: Jesus had a whole lot of nerve!

Unplug Your Mind: What do you make of a Jesus that commands you to neglect your obligations to the traditions and expectations of where you were raised?

Jesus Rejects a Man's Proposal to Seize Power

Some people assumed Jesus would get rid of the Romans. This is common knowledge today, and many—if not most—scholars support this idea. *I'll follow you wherever you go,* said one enthusiastic young man. Everyone knew Jesus was on his way to Jerusalem, and it is not a stretch to hear in this young man's enthusiasm a willingness to fight, even die, for the nationalist cause.

> "As they were walking along the road, a man said to him, 'I will follow you wherever you go.' Jesus replied, 'Foxes have holes and birds of the air have nests, but the Son of Man has no place to lay his head'" (Lk 9:57–58, NIV).

It is interesting how Jesus handles him. And if we did not know that "foxes" and "birds of the air" were nicknames from that time period, we might have missed Jesus's meaning. *Foxes have holes, and birds of the air have nests. But the Son of Man has no place to lay his head.* He could be merely warning the would-be follower of the difficulty of life on the road. But there is more to it.

If someone in first century Judaism was called a *fox,* it was because he was a Jew (even if he was only part Jewish by blood, or a non-practicing Jew—Herod the Great fit both categories) who fraternized with the enemy. To put it simply, we are talking about someone who sold out, a traitor and an opportunist: someone like the Herods (Herod the Great, Herod Antipas, Herod Philip, etc., all who worked for Rome).

Jesus once called Antipas by this nickname: He said to them, "Go and tell that *fox* for me, Listen, I am casting out demons and performing cures today and tomorrow, and on the third day I finish my work" (Lk 13:32, NRSV [italics mine]). Likewise, if someone referred to *birds of the air* in first century Judaism, he could be referring to any Gentile nation, most certainly including Rome,[2] whose national symbol was an eagle.

The phrase "birds of the air" in the Bible refers almost exclusively to large soaring birds: vultures, eagles, hawks, and so on. For example, in 2 Samuel 21:10, Rizpah, one of Saul's widows, guarded the impaled bodies of her sons from scavenging animals: "She did not allow the *birds of the air* to come on the bodies by day, or the wild animals by night" (NRSV [italics mine]). The phrase also appears in one of Jesus's most memorable parables:

> "The kingdom of heaven is like a mustard seed that someone took and sowed in his field; it is the smallest of all the seeds, but when it has grown it is the greatest of shrubs and becomes a tree, so that the *birds of the air* come and make nests in its branches" (Mt 13:31–32, NRSV [italics mine]).

Sparrows would hardly make the point; they can and do nest in little bushes. But if the tiny seed grows to a tree large enough for an Imperial Eagle to make its nest in, then the point is well made. So this powerful Imperial Eagle, one of the Mediterranean's many soaring birds of prey—or one of the soaring *birds of the air,* as the Jews called it—made a nice metaphorical nickname for Rome.

Applying this knowledge of nicknames to what Jesus said to this young man, what meaning can we glean? *Foxes have holes,* he said. That is, a fraternizer with Rome knows how to secure his place, to furnish his den, like Herod. *Birds of the air have nests,* he said. That is, the Gentile nations—especially Rome—know how to secure their place, to feather their nest. Maybe Jesus was saying, *If you want to secure your place, your prestige, your popularity, go with the foxes. They know how to dig out their cozy little dens. Or go with the soaring birds. They know how to feather and defend their own nests. But the Son of Man is not interested in these things. He is coming to give up security—to give up power, prestige, and popularity. He has no place to lay his head.*

In plain English, Jesus was saying to the young man, *If you are volunteering for a revolution, go home. If you are asking to partici-*

pate in a coup, my answer is No. This is not about saving Israel from the Romans by force. It is about showing the world a kingdom that again and again it does not understand—one where power, prestige, and popularity are renounced, and one where guarded, security-seeking politics is rejected. If you want to storm Jerusalem, the answer is No. Absolutely No. I go there not to take life, but to give it.

These three refusals from Luke's Gospel (see also Mt 8:19–21) belong together, and again they are here sequentially in the reverse order that they appear in Luke. In the original order, Jesus said No to the revolutionary who loves his country, No to the community-minded fellow, then No to the mama's boy who needs parental permission.

Each of them could have been useful to Jesus and the kingdom, yet all three were enmeshed in systems with high expectations. Those expectations were, specifically, to be loyal to country, loyal to community, and loyal to family.

Did any of them break away to follow him? Luke never says. We will never know. But perhaps that is not the point. Maybe the point is that we are faced with the same choices.

Unplug Your Mind: Can you think of a time when your loyalty to your country, your community, or your family conflicted with your loyalty to Jesus? *Yes putting 1st Family — younger Days — 09.09*

Jesus Refuses to Defend His Authority to Judean Authorities

He has said No to followers. Now he says No to foes.

After Jesus's near riot-causing ride on a donkey into Jerusalem, Jesus entered the temple with his entourage. There he destroyed the currency exchange tables, wrecked the market, drove out merchants and animals, stationed his people at the entrances to keep worshipers from entering or leaving carrying anything, and began to teach (Mk 11:15–17; Mt 21:12–13, Lk 19:45–46, and Jn 2:13–22). He chided them, saying, "Is it not written: 'My house shall be called a house of prayer for all peoples'? But you have made it a den of thieves" (Mk 11:17, NAB).

Then he came back the next day and took over the place again, challenging the temple authorities on their own turf! (Mk 11:27; Mt 21:23). It was risky, but apparently the people liked what Jesus was doing. And their approval provided him with some measure of cover, at least then. "They wanted to arrest him, but they feared the crowds, because they regarded him as a prophet" (Mt 21:46, NRSV). Because Jesus had captured the attention of the crowds, his imminent arrest was delayed.

"The chief priests, the scribes, and the leaders of the people kept looking for a way to kill him; but they did not find anything they could do, for all the people were spellbound by what they heard" (Lk 19:47b–48, NRSV).

Yet, as you might expect, the chief priests, scribes, and elders were ready for him the second day, and they had prepared a question to test the Galilean rabbi (Mt 21:23–27). *By what authority are you doing these things?* they asked Jesus. *Who authorized you to do them?* (based on Mt 21:23b).

Of course it was a trap. The elders thought they had him either way. If he said his authority came from "men," they would ask, *With whom did you study? What is your title? Where are your credentials? Where is your office?* But on the other hand, if Jesus claimed his authority came from God, they were ready to challenge his origins and his behavior: *Can anything good come from Nazareth? Why do you break the Sabbath? Why do you consort with known sinners? If your authority was from God, you would not be from Galilee and you would not be a lawbreaker.*

We can assume that Jesus had no intention of being lured into this trap. He would not waste his time in a debate with phonies who would never believe he was sent from God. So he took charge by posing a question to them to expose their hypocrisy:

He said, *I have a question for you, just one. Answer it and I'll tell you by what authority I have taken this temple. Are you ready? Here it is: Did the baptism of John come from God, or was it a human invention?*

What happened next must have been a delight to behold. The elders started caucusing while Jesus and the crowd awaited their ruling. They immediately realized they were stuck. Bested already. They could not say John's baptism came from God, because Jesus would say, *Well why didn't you believe him?* They could not say it was merely human, because the people believed in John, and they were afraid of what the people might think, or say, or do. Being cowards and hypocrites, they were unwilling to do battle with Jesus on those terms. So . . .

The elders did the safe thing and agreed to respond, *We don't know.* Then Jesus struck the coup de grace: "Neither will I tell you by what authority I am doing these things" (Mt 21:27, NIV). He refused to answer.

Amazing. Called on the carpet by the biggest of the big cheeses, and Jesus stood them down. They were bested by a Galilean bumpkin. Jim Fleming, a biblical scholar and teacher in Israel, once called Jesus "a hard-hat from Podunk."[3] The elders must have been thunderstruck. They had their hands full with the rabbi from Nazareth. Now they were thinking, *We've got trouble, right here in River City. This Jesus has our number. And he knows it.*

But Jesus didn't stop there. He did not even give them a chance to breathe. He shot a question straight at them: *What do you think? A man had two sons, and he told the first one to go work in the vineyard. The son refused, but later changed his mind and went. Then to the second son the man said the same thing, and that son said, "Yes, sir. Right away, sir." But then he didn't go. Which son did the will of his father? They said, "The first one."* Jesus said, "I tell you the truth, the tax collectors and the prostitutes are entering the kingdom of God ahead of you" (Mt 21:28–32, NIV).

Then he hammered them again with a second parable: *There was a landowner who planted a vineyard, put a fence around it, dug a wine press in it, and built a watchtower. Then he leased it to some tenants and went to his second home in another country. When the harvest time came, he sent his slaves to the tenants to collect his produce. But the tenants grabbed his slaves and beat one, killed another, and stoned another. Again he sent more slaves; and they treated them the same way. Finally he sent his son to them, saying to himself, "They will have to respect my son." But when the tenants saw the son, they said to themselves, "Look, here is the heir; let's kill him and get his inheritance!" So they grabbed him, threw him out of the vineyard, and killed him. Now when the owner of the vineyard comes, what will he do to those tenants?* It was a rhetorical question, and Jesus answered it himself: *He will put those wretches to a miserable death, and lease the vineyard to other tenants who will give him his produce at the harvest time like they are supposed to do!* Then to make sure and drive the point home, Jesus said to them, *Have you never read in the Scriptures: "The stone that the builders rejected has become the cornerstone; this was the Lord's doing, and it is amazing in our eyes"? Therefore the kingdom of God will be taken away from you and given to a people that produces the fruits of the kingdom* (from Mt 21:33-44, NRSV).

By the time the chief priests and the Pharisees realized he was telling parables against them, it was too late. The people were laughing and cheering and they dared not arrest him. So he hit them with a third parable: *The kingdom of heaven is like a king who gave a wedding banquet for his son. He sent his slaves to call those who had been invited to the wedding banquet, but they wouldn't come. He sent other slaves, saying, 'Tell everyone I've invited: Look, I have prepared my dinner, my oxen and my fat calves have been barbequed, and everything is ready; come to the wedding banquet.' But they made fun of them and went away, one to his farm, another to his business, while the rest seized his slaves, mistreated them, and killed them. The king was enraged. He sent his troops, destroyed those murderers, and burned their city. Then he said to his slaves, 'The wedding is ready, but the ones I invited blew it. So go downtown and invite everyone you run into.' Those slaves went out into the streets and gathered everyone they could find, both good and bad until the wedding hall was filled with guests* (based on Mt 22:1–14).

Jesus must have stunned the temple authorities. He did not turn out to be the simple, demure, traveling evangelist they expected. Debating him was not going to be easy, especially while he was surrounded by his adoring fans. Jesus had made the leaders look foolish, and he had insulted them in front of the people. But they did not give up, not by a long shot. They merely lost round one. Time to strategize a new fight plan.

Round two. The Pharisees saw the thrashing that the chief priests and elders took, and they called an emergency meeting to figure out a strategy to derail Jesus. They came back with a test about taxes to Caesar. They tried to set him up with flattery and a trick question: *Teacher, we know that you are sincere, and teach the way of God in accordance with truth, and show favoritism to no one; for you do not treat people with partiality. Tell us, then, what you think. Is it lawful to pay taxes to the emperor, or not?* (based on Mt 22:15–22). Obviously this was another trap. If he said it was lawful to pay taxes to the emperor, then they could brand him a Roman collaborator, no better than a tax collector. If he said it was unlawful, then they could accuse him of being anti-Roman, a troublemaker, another Galilean zealot. They figured they had him either way. Jesus's response amazed them and sent them away baffled and defeated.

He said, *Why are you hypocrites testing me? Bring me the tax coin. Whose face is on this thing? Whose name? Then give Caesar back his coin, but give to God what is God's* (challenge, then responding insult and riposte). He exposed their malice and directed the people to give themselves wholly to God—mind, body, and spirit.

Round three. Some Sadducees came in with a test about resurrection and marriage, and they got clobbered. *Teacher, Moses said, "If a man dies childless, his brother has to marry the widow, and raise up children for his brother." Now there were seven brothers; the first married and died childless, leaving the wodow to his brother. The second did the same; so also the third, down to the seventh. Then last of all, the woman herself died. So in the resurrection, whose wife will she be?"* [**FYI**: Sadducees did not believe in resurrection.] Quick as a lick, Jesus knocked them silly: *You are wrong, because you don't know the Bible and you don't know the power of God, he said. First of all, marriage is irrelevant in the resurrection. Second of all, if God is the God of Abraham, and God is the God of the living and not the dead, then there must be a resurrection* (based on Mt 22:23–33).

Matthew says the crowd was absolutely astounded, and the Sadducees had no choice but to leave in humiliation.

Round four. When the Pharisees realized that the Sadducees had been bested, they saw this as a twofold opportunity. They thought, *If we can go back and best Jesus now, we can also show all the people that we Pharisees are smarter than the Sadducees!*

They rushed in to seize the moment. However, they made a massive strategic blunder. They asked Jesus the question to end all questions: *What is the greatest commandment?* He quoted Deuteronomy and Leviticus: *Love God and love your neighbor. Every other law hangs on these* (based on Mt 22:34–40).

Round five. The Pharisees could not argue with that, so they just stood there not knowing what to do. Jesus goes on the offensive again. *What's your take on the Messiah?* he asked them. *Whose son is he?* Easy question, the Pharisees thought. *He's the son of David*, they said. *Wrong!* Jesus replied. *If the Messiah is David's son, then how is it that in Psalm 110 David refers to the Messiah as Lord?* (based on Mt 22:42–45) Then, as Matthew writes, "No one could think of anything to say in reply, and from that day no one dared to ask him any further questions" (Mt 22:46, NJB).

No one dared. His opponents reeled and fell to the canvas.

But guess what? Jesus did not stop. Some well dressed scribes were still standing there. So he hit them when they were not looking! He announced to all in a loud voice, "Beware the scribes, who like to walk around in long robes, and to be greeted with respect in the marketplaces, and to have the best seats in the synagogues and places of honor at banquets. They devour widows' houses and for the sake of appearance say long prayers. They will receive the greater condemnation" (Mk 12:38–40, NRSV).

He did not just deck them. He destroyed them, right there in their own back yard! Knock out, fifth round. Somebody call an ambulance.

Whatever happened to the pensive, wimpy Jesus so many of us learned about in Sunday school? Where is the frail, ethereal savior we have always known?

To recap: *No,* Jesus said, *I will not tell you by what authority I do these things.* He knew the temple leaders to be hypocrites and blind guides, and it was useless to dialogue with them. They were threatened by his spirit, his freedom, and his power. This is why they were afraid of him:

"I've already told you, and you don't believe. You've seen with your own eyes the mighty works I do in God's name, and you don't believe. Your ears and eyes do not work. If they did, you would know that the Father and I are one." They picked up stones to kill him, but Jesus asked, "You've seen me do many great things; which one are you stoning me for?" (based on Jn 10:24–32).

Now that is spirit and freedom and power!

Unplug Your Mind: If you had the nerve, the ability, and the opportunity to expose the hypocrisy or bad theology of religious leaders publicly, where would you do it, how would you do it, and what would you say?

Jesus Refuses to Perform Signs as Proof

People asked Jesus to *perform*—that is the operative word—a sign to give proof of who he was. All four Gospels offer at least one example each of this, giving the impression that it happened often during his ministry. (Mt 12:38, 16:1; Mk 8:11, Lk 11:16, 23:8; Jn 2:18, 6:30) Even Herod, while Jesus was on trial, wanted Jesus to put on a show for him. "When Herod saw Jesus, he was greatly pleased, because for a long time he had been wanting to see him. From what he had heard about him, he hoped to see him perform a sign of some sort" (Lk 23:8, TNIV). The musical, *Jesus Christ Superstar*, picks up on this when the character Herod Antipas sings:

> *"Show me now that you're no fool,*
> *walk across my swimming pool."* [4]

Jesus refused Herod. Moreover, Jesus refused every request for a sign, and it bothered him a lot that people kept expecting him to do tricks.

Some Pharisees came to argue with him and to test him by asking him for a sign from heaven (Mk 8:11–12). This bugged Jesus. His response was visceral. Mark says he "sighed deeply in his spirit," which is Mark's way of saying Jesus was exasperated, verging on anger. *Why, why, why do you people keep wanting a sign?* he asked. *I'll tell you what. Here is the bottom line: No sign, not a single blessed one, will you get.*

He said No, and walked away.

Sign-seekers got nothing from Jesus. Why? What was the big deal?

John explains it this way: A lot of people were believing in Jesus because of various signs he performed. Either they heard about miracles or saw them firsthand. But Jesus did not trust them because, as John says, he knew human nature all too well (Jn 2:23-25). No one had to explain it to him. Jesus knew what made people tick, and we are not really that different today. People crave the sensational. They love Elvis and O.J. and Madonna and Princess Di and JFK and MLK and Robert Blake and Kobe and Jacko and Liz and Farrakhan and Jessie and Monica and Clinton and Tommy and Pamela and Paris and Pee Wee and on and on ... . You get the picture. It is the cult of personality. People want a *performing* messiah, a front stage center TV evangelist with big hair to put on a big show. The most well known televangelists are nothing if not show-men and women. They have to be. They know that very few of their contributors are interested primarily in "a message." Many mega-preachers give the desperate masses what they want: emotionalism, sensationalism, and theatrics. We can assume the early followers of Jesus were looking for the same kind of spectacle. *So, forget the message. Wow me, Jesus!*

However, if someone believed in him because of the signs he performed, fine. That was an OK place to start, Jesus said (Jn 10:38). But the signs point to who he is, to the Word of God made flesh (Jn 1:1–3, 14), to his glory in the cross. Yet, true followers didn't need proof. "Blessed are those who have not seen and have believed" (Jn 20:29, NAB). Signs were not necessary for faith; sometimes they helped, but sometimes they got in the way.

Jesus said, "This generation is evil and adulterous. No sign will be given to an evil and adulterous generation but the sign of Jonah. For just as the prophet was in the belly of a sea monster for three days and three nights, so the Son of Man will be in the earth" (based on Mt 12:38–40).

In other words, the only sign necessary was his death and resurrection. It is the only sign sufficient for life and faith. Not much else matters, and any so-called sign that does not point to that is false.

It is faith—not superstition, not sensationalism, not magic, not showmanship—that saves. Faith in the Word of God, in Jesus himself, is the true message. The Word is manifest in the flesh in the person of Jesus; it dies and rises, defeating sin and death. Everything else is either bonus or bogus. [**FYI:** Notice that the Bible never refers to itself as the "Word of God." The Bible calls *Jesus* the Word of God (Jn 1:1-3, 14). The Word is a living *person*, not paper and ink. Jesus said, **"**You pore over the scriptures, believing that in them you can find eternal life; it is these scriptures that testify to me, and yet you refuse to come to me to receive life! (Jn 5:39–40, NJB).

Whenever he was asked for a proof, no matter who asked, no matter when, and no matter where, Jesus had only one answer: *No.*

Unplug Your Mind: Think of someone you love: How would you go about *proving* your love to him or her?

Jesus Refuses Satan's Three Tempting Alternatives

We conclude this chapter with Jesus's most important collection of Nos, back at the very beginning of his ministry—his baptism and temptations in the wilderness. The importance of this cannot be overstated. This was when he said No to Satan. Three times. These Nos are the backbone of every No discussed so far, and every No to follow.

The tempter came to Jesus and said "If you are the Son of God, command these stones to become loaves of bread." But he answered, "It is written, 'One does not live by bread alone, but by every word that comes from the mouth of God.'" Then the devil took him to the holy city and placed him on the pinnacle of the temple, saying to him, "If you are the Son of God, throw yourself down; for it is written, 'He will command his angels concerning you,' and 'On their hands they will bear you up, so that you will not dash your foot against a stone.'" Jesus said to him, "Again it is written, 'Do not put the Lord your God to the test.'" Again, the devil took him to a very high mountain and showed him all the kingdoms of the world and their splendor; and he said to him, "All these I will give you, if you will fall down and worship me." Jesus said to him, "Away with you, Satan! for it is written, 'Worship the Lord your God, and serve only him'" (Mt 4:3–10, NRSV). But the context of this testing is critical. Let's back up. It was the Spirit of the Father, not Satan, Mark says, that drove the Son into the Judean desert to be tested (Mk 1:12). Jesus's testing is a result not of an experience of rejection, but of God's *affirmation* at his baptism: "You are my beloved Son with whom I am well pleased" (Lk 3:22). Those who think rejection is more difficult to handle than affirmation should think again. Jesus was affirmed by God, and immediately the Spirit shoved him into the wild for an intense and lengthy struggle. *I'm God's Son. He's pleased with me. Now what?*

So it was the Voice of God that created this crisis! It was the Spirit of God that drove him into the desert to stumble around for a few weeks of grueling mental and physical strain. That was when temptation came.

During these trials of temptation, Jesus considered turning stones to bread. Is this merely because he was hungry, or does this represent his temptation to make the focus of his Sonship economics—the eradication of hunger worldwide? Imagine. No more hunger.

He considered leaping from the pinnacle of the temple in Jerusalem. Is this merely because he was tempted by personal fame and glory, or does this symbolize a "religious" messianic rule where people have no choice but to be unified in belief because of his overwhelming demonstrations of power? Imagine. No more religious strife.

He considered worshiping the "ruler of this world" in order to possess it. Is this personal political ambition, or is this about a military rule that eliminates war, inaugurating world peace? Imagine. No more war.

Let us assume the latter in each case, that Jesus was tempted to end world hunger, religious strife, and all war. The temptations then had to do with the focus and direction of his messiahship. Any or all of these could have yielded untold good. He was quite seriously tempted to do three things, all of which were in his power to do, all of which could have yielded unparalleled benefits for humanity (no hunger, no conflicts of faith, no war). *We are tempted to do the things we can do, not the things we cannot.*[5] That is why Satan's temptations were so insidious for Jesus. All of these were within his reach, and all could have been of great benefit to the world. So why did he say No?

We cannot be completely certain why he rejected the three options that tempted him. But we have clues from the Scriptures he quoted. "A human does not live by bread alone"(Mt 4:4; Lk 4:4). "Do not test God" (Mt 4:7; Lk 4:12). "Worship and serve God only" (Mt 4:10; Lk 4:8). There was something about Satan's three options that, while tempting, did not jibe with Scripture, and, in the end, Jesus rejected them. Bread is not primary. Testing God shows a lack of faith. Worshiping anyone or anything other than God leads to no good. So Scripture became his strength and his voice during the time of testing. Christians would do well to remember that.

While Jesus did not make feeding the world the focus of his ministry, nevertheless he fed the 5,000 and he gave alms. While he did not leap from the pinnacle of the temple to use his power to coerce, he nonetheless performed works of power, mostly healings, done almost always in private, followed by orders of secrecy. And while he did not choose to be a military leader inaugurating world peace, he threw himself into battle against evil, those forces (meteorological, biological, and psychological) that maim and destroy life. But all of these, the feeding, the healing, the battling, were all subordinated to his primary mission: "Let us go on to the nearby villages that I may preach there also. For this purpose have I come" (Mk 1:38, NAB).

Jesus turned down the chance to become an economic, religious, and military messiah. Satan offered him all three. To all three Jesus said *No*. Instead, he chose teaching. It was his Father's will that he proclaim the good news of the Kingdom. He made that the main thing.

Unplug Your Mind: Have you ever deliberately avoided doing good for a higher purpose?

Conclusion

To disciples trying to help feed a throng he said No. To would-be followers with wrongheaded priorities, he said No. To opponents who tested him and demanded proof, he said No. And to Satan's three alternate paths, no matter the potential good they might yield, he said No.

Beware when all speak well of you, Jesus said, *for your ancestors all spoke well of the false prophets* (based on Lk 6:26). This quote was placed beneath the title of this chapter for a reason. You are in grave spiritual danger if all speak well of you. The only way to possibly get everyone to speak well of you is to *always* say what others want to hear, and *never* say No to demands and requests. Are there not enough "yes men" in the world? Why then do so many Christians spend so much time and energy worrying about what others will say? Why are we so hellbent on being likable and popular? Just because everyone likes you does not make you a Christian. Following Jesus does not prove your likeability. If you want popularity and universal praise, perhaps Jesus is not the one to follow. Likeability, popularity, and universal praise are not what got him killed!

Beware when all speak well of you, because the only time when all speak well of you is when you are not following him, when you are not taking stands, when you are not making a difference, when you avoid disappointing, when you refuse to say Yes and No and mean both, and when you stray from his courageous, narrow path of truth and life. To follow him is to assure that all will not—I repeat—*will not* speak well of you. Yes, Jesus was hated by many (and still is), but he said, *If the world hates you, remember it hated me first* (Jn 15:18). In other words, you are in good company. *There is a lot of trouble in the world,* he said, *but be courageous, because I have conquered the world* (based on Jn 16:33b).

We have looked at Jesus's refusals of acquaintances. We have looked at his refusals of followers and foes alike. But are you aware that he even said No to his family?

3

HE SAID NO TO HIS FAMILY

"Who are my mother and brothers?"

—Mark 3:33

No to acquaintances? Necessary apparently. No to followers and foes alike? Understandable. But why in the world would our New Testament gospels record Jesus saying No to his own family members? To his kin in Nazareth, to his brothers, and more than once to his own mother, Jesus said No. It is critical that we look openly and honestly at why.

Jesus Rejects His Hometown's Expectations

When Jesus returned to his hometown synagogue in Nazareth (Lk 4:16–30), after having begun his Galilean ministry based in Capernaum, he was well aware of what his kin there expected to see and hear.

First, they were impressed with his choice of Scripture. From Isaiah he read, "The Spirit of the Lord is upon me, because he has anointed me to proclaim good news to the poor. He has sent me to proclaim release to the captives and the regaining of sight to the blind, to set free those who are oppressed, to proclaim the year of the Lord's favor" (Lk 4:18–19). After Jesus moved the crowd with his words, they asked among themselves, *Isn't this Joseph's boy?*

In spite of the accolades, however, he then let them know that he was very conscious of why they all turned out and what they were expecting. They wanted their favorite son to declare that he had been sent to *them* (that is, Nazareth, and perhaps to all of Israel!) as the Messiah, and they assumed he would do here in his hometown the great things that he had done for the "riffraff" in Capernaum, even greater things. But what they never expected was that he might refuse to do either. No declarations. No demonstrations.

Nothing was in store for Nazareth that day except a scalding truth. (Mt 13:58 records that he *would* not do many deeds of power. Mk 6:5 records that he *could* not.) Jesus read their minds. They were quoting to him in their minds, "Physician, heal *yourself*," meaning, Jesus, you've done great things elsewhere; now do your greatest miracles for your own hometown kin. But Jesus countered those expectations, proclaiming that prophets get honor everywhere but their own hometowns. (Lk 4:23–24) That comment must have felt to them like a cold slap in the face.

As though he had not said enough already, Jesus then went on to explain in not so many words, *Not only am I not going to do diddly for you, but God is not going to do diddly for you either!* He reminded them that Elijah went to a widow in Sidon instead of any of the widows of Israel during a famine. And he reminded them that Elisha cleansed the leprosy of a Syrian rather than any leper of Israel (1 Kgs 17:1, 8–16; 18:1; 2 Kgs 5:1–14). Jesus told them, in other words, *When you start expecting favoritism from God, you are in for a rude awakening* (based on Lk 4:25–28).

Jesus disappointed them by refusing to do great things in Nazareth, by refusing to say what they wanted to hear about their specialness to God, and by refusing to pander to them so that he could be their hometown boy who made it big. He most certainly disappointed them. But he went beyond mere refusal. He quoted their own Scriptures against them, using the heroes Elijah and Elisha to send the clear message that God had chosen *other* people to bless, *not them*. Nazareth was to get nothing. They were enraged (Lk 4:28).

A person could be stoned by using one of two methods: Throw rocks on the person, or throw the person on rocks! Jesus's kin, the people of his childhood and growing-up years, drove him out of town to a cliff to throw him off, but he managed to "pass through the midst of them."

"He came to what was his own, and his own people did not accept him" (Jn 1:11, NRSV).

Unplug Your Mind: Under what circumstances would you be willing to tell loved ones exactly what they don't want to hear?

Jesus Says No to His Mother

As difficult as it may be to admit, it is a fact according to the Gospels that whenever Mary or his brothers came around, Jesus said No to them! As strange as it seems, Jesus detached himself quite intentionally from his family. The No in the Nazareth synagogue, it should be remembered, was Jesus's refusal to perform for his kin. [**FYI:** Scholarship supports strongly the conclusion that Nazareth was a small clan, from the lineage of David, who lived in isolation in mountainside houses built on top and in front of caves; i.e., most—if not all—villagers were related.] These kin turned into a lynch mob; they tried to execute him.

The Scriptures do not say Mary and his brothers or sisters were there for the attempted stoning, but they no doubt were. Certainly they would not have missed his return or his appearance in the synagogue, since their absence would have been conspicuous in a village of 200 to 500 men, women, and children.[1] We can only hope that his mother, brothers, and sisters did not participate in the riot that followed, but the Gospels do not say one way or the other. However, think of

the repercussions even if they did not take part. Jesus was dead
to Nazareth and could never return. Mary and his brothers
and sisters had to live with the humiliation and the grief. We
know that they continued to care for him from afar and from
time to time they made contact beyond Nazareth, the city
limits of which Jesus, so far as we know, never again entered.

So Mary and the brothers continued to see Jesus after
he was run out of Nazareth, but only because they went to
where he was, or they happened to be at the same place at the
same time as he, as was the case with the wedding at Cana.

John 2:1–11 tells us there was a wedding in Cana, Jesus's
mother was there, and, as it turns out, Jesus and his disciples
were also invited. By this time Jesus was living in Capernaum
(Mk 2:1). He traveled from there to Cana with his disciples.
His mother traveled from Nazareth. Geographically it is un-
likely that they came to Cana together. And John makes it
very plain that they did not. He writes, "Mary was there." He
continues, "Jesus and his disciples had also been invited."

Then there was a social catastrophe, at least in that culture,
if not in our own: The wine gave out. *They have run out of wine*,
Mary said to her son. Her comment may have merely been
an observation. Or perhaps she was in charge of the food and
drink by request of the groom's family and it was her fault the
wine ran out, or at least her responsibility to try to get more.
More likely, however, it was not her responsibility at all; she
had merely become anxious over the embarrassing problem
she was witnessing, and she was over-functioning. She said to
Jesus, "They have no more wine," implying that maybe we
(you) should do something.

"Woman, what concern is that to you and to me?" (Jn 2:4a,
NRSV) was Jesus's reply to his mother.

"Woman" was a respectful and common title to use, but
a son would not normally use it in reference to his own
mother.[2] Jesus called her an everyday title that he might call
any woman. Was Jesus making a point by addressing her as

such? Now that he was a grown man, she was just a "woman?" Now that he had left home and had begun his ministry, she was merely like any other "woman" to him; was she not his mother anymore? We simply do not have enough information to be sure why Jesus called her this. We do not know when he began to address her in this way, or why, or whether it hurt her feelings. But Jesus continued to speak to her on this occasion, and it is difficult to miss the brusqueness of his comment to Mary or the distance it witnesses to.

Don't miss it. He was saying No to his mom. The wine was not his problem, he said. Jesus was refusing to get involved, and he was telling her that *her* involvement was inappropriate. This was not her family. This was not her affair. She should stay out of it. She was not the caterer, and he was not the bartender!

The story might have ended there. But Jesus made an additional comment that lets us know that even more was at stake. Still speaking to his mother and perhaps to others, he said, "My hour has not yet come" (Jn 2:4b, NRSV). There was no way she or anyone else understood what he meant.

What is Jesus's hour, and what does this have to do with a catering crisis? Jesus's hour is a repeated theme in John's Gospel. It is the hour of his passion, that is, his suffering unto death. What does his suffering have to do with wine running out at a wedding? In John, it has *everything* to do with it.

At Jesus's crucifixion, the pinnacle of his hour, moments after his death, much is made of the spear thrust into his side by a Roman soldier. Out came water and blood. John portrays this as a representation of the sacraments of baptism and communion. The way John emphasizes it, the water and blood coming out of his side is the most important crucifixion detail of them all. He wrote in Chapter 19, verses 34 to 35: "One of the soldiers pierced his side with a spear, and at once blood and water came out. (He who saw this has testified so that you also may believe. His testimony is true, and he knows that he tells the truth.)" (NRSV)

Jesus's turning water to wine, then, was about to become a *sign*, an intentional gesture on Jesus's part, pointing to his glory, his death, the moment when water and blood would pour from his own body.

Now it should make sense what he said: *It is not yet my hour.* It was not yet time for blood and water. Something as mundane as the absence of wine at a wedding became an opportunity for him to act symbolically, deliberately fore-shadowing his own death by changing water to wine. John calls them signs (σημεῖον—*semeion* in Greek), not miracles (δύναμις —*dunamis*, the root for our English words dynamic, dynamo, and dynamite) as in the other Gospels. And like all signs, they point beyond themselves. They point to the glory of God to be revealed in Jesus's passion—his suffering. Always in John's Gospel, Jesus's suffering and death is God's glory. That is the great paradox. The glory is in the giving of his life, pouring out his blood as a holy sacrifice, a sacrament of body, blood, and water. "Father, the time has come. Glorify your Son, that your Son may glorify you" (Jn 17:1b, NIV).

So Jesus's refusal to cater a wedding is still intact! He did not change water to wine for that purpose at all. His purpose, as always, was to foretell the glory of God: his hour of sacri-fice. Rescuing the wedding from winelessness was merely the *opportunity*. Mary may have thought Jesus did it for her or for the sake of the wedding party, but that is simply not the case.

John reports an overlooked and misunderstood detail to ensure that we understand that Jesus's purpose was not merely to bartend a wedding banquet; Jesus ordered the servants to draw out some of the wine and take it to the chief stew-ard. When the man in charge tasted the wine, he complained, *Don't you fools know that you're supposed to serve the best wine first? Then you're supposed to serve the cheap stuff later after every-body's drunk and can't taste the difference! Why in the world did you keep the best stuff for last?* (based on Jn 2:10).

If Jesus's intent was to smooth out a catering problem, then he failed miserably! Because when the maitre d' tasted the fine wine, he was not amused. At that point the banquet had a new problem: The best wine was not served early. Now the host could be accused of being inhospitable.

But, if Jesus's intent was to perform a miracle as a sign, as is always the case in John's Gospel, what then does it symbolize? The water and wine of his approaching Last Supper, which in John's Gospel included a ceremonial foot-washing (Jn 13:1–11), and it points to his sacrificial death when water and blood flow from his side. If this was his intent at the wedding at Cana, then he hit a home run, although the perturbed head steward may not have agreed.

It may come as a shock that Jesus was not a do-gooder. At least in the gospel of John, he does not perform miracles or do favors out of compassion or sympathy, and he certainly doesn't do them on demand. Jesus He acts out of his Father's will and timing only—even when it could appear cruel, uncaring, or at least odd, as when it was reported that Lazarus ("the one whom you love") was very ill, *and Jesus stayed two days longer where he was!* (Jn 11:1-6).

It is true that Jesus's behavior and words sometimes baffled his disciples. But his family was baffled too. And the scriptural facts are that Jesus said No to his Nazareth kin in a sermon (Mt 13:54–58; Mk 6:1–6; Lk 4:16–30), and he said No to his mother at a wedding (Jn 2:1–11). And, as you will see in the following sections of this chapter, Jesus said No to his brother's well-meaning advice (Jn 7:1–10), and he said No to his mother and brothers' attempt to restrain him for fear that he was mentally ill (Mk 3:21–35). Yes, it is true. But those sections will have to wait while we ponder an important question now: If Mary or other family members in Nazareth were aware of Mary's visit from an angel and aware of Jesus's miraculous conception (Lk 1:26–38), aware of visiting shep-

herds speaking of more angels (Lk 2:8–20), aware of Sime-
on's prophesy and Anna's prophesy (Lk 2:21–38), aware of a
strange star and visiting Magi with rare gifts (Mt 2:1–12), and
aware of Joseph's dreams (Mt 1:18–25, 2:13–15, and 19–23),
then why did his family come to doubt the adult Jesus?

One would think that in light of visiting angels and wise
men attending Jesus's birth that Mary would fully understand,
believe, and appreciate whatever Jesus did or said, without
question. The same goes for his brothers, his sisters, and the
whole village of Nazareth. But, it didn't turn out that way.
Why?

A large part of it must have been that Jesus was just one
of them for so many years. Familiarity and proximity allowed
his kin to see him as only human—dirty diapers and teenage
pranks—and crowded out their memories and expectations,
though certainly not their hopes. In most ways, if not all ways,
he was a normal kid in the village.

We have in Scripture only one story from Jesus's childhood. When he was twelve, he not only scared Mary and
Joseph to death by remaining behind in the Jerusalem Temple
(Lk 2:41–51), but he smarted off when they found him: *You
should have known where I'd be—in my Father's house!*

That kind of behavior, the kind that gives parents heart
attacks, really *would* overshadow in time the heavenly mag-
nificence of angels and wise men. Years and years of everyday
family life could eaasily have cast shadows of doubt on special prophesies. Moreover, Jesus's own behavior led to their
doubting too. They actually came to doubt his sanity!

In spite of a miraculous conception and heavenly prom-
ises, Jesus's family came to have problems with the adult Jesus's
behavior and teachings. Matthew, Mark, Luke, and John all say
so. Each Gospel writer had every opportunity to cover up this
rather shocking fact, but none did. They told the truth. Jesus's
family had trouble with him. Also, say all four Gospels, Jesus

distanced himself from his family. These things will become clearer as we move to the next two refusals—both of them, as promised, refusals of his family.

Unplug Your Mind: Why is it troubling to think that Jesus did not always have a harmonious relationship with his mother?

Jesus Says No to His Brothers

Everybody has political advice. Jesus's brothers told him to go to the bright lights of the big city during an important festival for more exposure: *Show off the things you're doing here, Jesus, but do it where it will count for something. Nobody who wants to make a reputation for himself performs in secret. Do your stuff in the capital city; do it front and center in the temple, where all the right people will be impressed and believe in you. That's the kind of PR you need, brother* (based on Jn 7:3–4).

This is advice for anyone seeking publicity, popularity, or elected office. But Jesus was uninterested in these things, and John makes it clear that this advice was direct evidence that "not even his brothers believed in him" (Jn 7:5). What they proposed—a strategy to increase popularity—was diametrically opposed to God's will.

Ironically, Jesus had already rejected the temptation offered by Satan to leap from the pinnacle of the temple to prove to Jerusalem that he was the Son of God. It is a potentially painful realization that Jesus's brothers try to tempt him with essentially the same advice Satan proffered: *Show off in Jerusalem and prove to Jerusalem who you are* (based on Mt 4:5–6; Lk 4:9–11).

Jesus's response is predictable, given his prior rejection of a similar suggestion made by Satan (not to mention this chapter's title). *Go up to the festival yourselves,* he said to them. *I'm not going up to this festival, for my time has not fully come* (based on Jn 7:8).

So, he refused his brothers and their savvy political advice. Nobody runs things for Jesus but God. In John's Gospel, Father and Son are one, of one mind and one will (Jn 10:30, 17:11).

It is important to remember we are reading John. Here, Jesus does absolutely nothing because of the prompting of others. He acts in God's good time and no one else's, at all times and in all circumstances. His "time" or "hour" is between him and God and not scheduled by anyone else. He is free from the demands of others. He has an internal Counselor. No other counsel matters.

So what does a discussion of travel to the temple have to do with Jesus's time and hour? It is language again that is the clue. Jesus told them to "go up," meaning to the festival. But it was not yet time for Jesus to "go up," referring to the time when he would be "lifted up," meaning on the cross. And when he does "go up," it will not be the Festival of Booths, but the Festival of the Passover.

Jesus was not lying when he said he had no plans to "go up," and then went. Look at the story closely. Jesus used the phrases "go up" and "my time." While he did end up going to Jerusalem behind his brothers when they thought he meant not to, it is another example in John's Gospel of Jesus speaking symbolically—and people hearing him literally—as when he said to the woman at the well, *If you knew who I was, you'd ask me for living water welling up to eternal life*; and she said, *Sir, this well is deep and you don't have a bucket!* (based on Jn 4:10–11).

When he said to his brothers that it was not yet his *time* to *go up*, he referred to the cross. What looks like a lie on the surface is an example of Jesus expressing a deeper meaning completely missed by his heedless brothers.

Jesus rejected at least three things when he answered his brothers' request. He rejected their prompting to attend the festival. He rejected the timing, because it was not yet the *hour*

for him to *go up*. And he rejected their advice to "show the
world what you can do." These were not compatible with his
Father's way and will. So, brothers or not, he said No.

[**FYI:** There is little agreement in the Christian world
about Jesus's brothers and sisters. Most modern liberal scholars
who reject the virgin birth of Jesus believe that Jesus's brothers and sisters were full brothers and sisters, all younger than
him, and all the offspring of Joseph and Mary. Most protestant
Christians affirm the virgin birth, and they think of Jesus's
brothers and sisters as *half* brothers and sisters, since Mary is
his mother, and God, not Joseph, is his Father; they too see
the siblings as younger than Jesus. Some Roman Catholics
and Eastern Orthodox Christians, who believe not only in
the virgin birth but also in the perpetual virginity of Mary,
believe that Jesus's brothers were all older stepbrothers and
stepsisters, the products of Joseph's supposed previous marriage, making Mary the biological mother of only one child
in the family—Jesus. Other Catholics and Orthodox Christians believe that his brothers and sisters were actually only
cousins. The "brothers'" names were James, Joseph (or Joses),
Simon, and Judas (Mt 13:55; Mk 6:3). His sisters are not mentioned by name in Scripture, nor do the Scriptures say how
many "sisters" he had.

The most revealing and clarifying scriptural statement
about Jesus's siblings is this: "When Joseph awoke from sleep,
he did as the angel of the Lord commanded him; he took
[Mary] as his wife, but had no marital relations with her *until*
she had borne a son; and he named him Jesus" (Mt 1:24–25,
NRSV [italics mine]).]

Unplug Your Mind: Which is ruder, trying to run your brother's life, or preventing him from running yours?

Jesus Says No to His Mother and His Brothers

Possession and insanity are commonly paired in the Gospels. For example, the man called Legion in Mark 5 was described as both demon possessed and insane. Then, after Jesus cast out the demons, Legion was back to his right mind. So in Jesus's day demon possession and insanity were linked. Demon possession caused insanity. Like it or not, many people, including Jesus's family began to wonder whether Jesus was insane: [His] family ... went to take charge of him, for they said, "He is out of his mind" (Mk 3:21, Today's NIV).

Is this news to you? People were saying Jesus was beside himself, out of his mind. His family concluded that he needed to be confronted—what we now call an "intervention." They considered restraining him, putting him away—what we call today "committing." It was probably their intention to do this quietly (Mt 1:19), so as to cause as little further embarrassment to the family as possible. Obviously, they were concerned for his safety and well-being, yet, as in all situations like this, families cannot help but also be concerned about their own reputations.

Of course Jesus's enemies accused him of insanity. That's to be expected. And they used the language of demon possession to do it. Not much of a stretch, culturally speaking. Presumably, they accused him of this regularly. Look at all the incidences recorded in the Gospels: Matthew 9:34, 10:25, 12:24; Mark 3:21–29; Luke 11:15–19; John 7:20, 8:48, 8:52; 10:20. The last one—John 10:20—explicitly pairs insanity with demon possession. It reads, "Many of them said, 'He is demon-possessed and raving mad. Why listen to him?'" (Jn 10:20, NIV).

But it was not only Jesus's enemies who questioned his sanity. Regular folks did, too, including his family (Mk 3:21). Interestingly, when this is mentioned by Bible teachers, someone in the class almost always challenges it. That's understandable. This portion of Scripture does not get a lot of exposure, as if *it* is an embarrassment itself. Admittedly, it is a disturbing episode. And without wider exposure through reading, preaching, and teaching, it remains unfamiliar. So, given that this passage exists, we might reasonably wonder *why* so many people, including his mother, were concerned that Jesus had lost his marbles.

Several of the things Jesus is reported to have done and said could have led them to question his sanity. Leaving Nazareth did not help, as he would have been perceived to be abandoning the specific family responsibilities an eldest son must fill, especially after the death of the father. (Joseph is presumed dead because he is never mentioned in Scripture after Luke 2:51 when Jesus was only twelve years old.)

But Jesus did not merely *leave* home—he was run out on a rail (Lk 4:29). To make matters worse, he moved to a much more cosmopolitan town on the highway and on the waterfront, Capernaum—quite an outlandish thing for an orthodox Nazarene to do. Jesus abandoned the rather strict, isolated ways of his hometown in favor of a very public lifestyle in a much more libertine community. Moreover, he associated with persons of disrepute regularly. He called together a tax collector, various fishermen, and a few revolutionaries to be his "disciples." He told parables that seemed to them to reject the Nazarene brand of Judaism. He did not wash his hands ritually, he did not fast weekly, he ate with the unclean when he wanted to, he traveled among Gentiles and Samaritans, and he constantly broke the Sabbath. Lastly, he treated them—his family—in ways that must have seemed disrespectful; he did not just leave home, but he distanced himself from them and refused them on numerous occasions.

To his family, insanity may have seemed a better explanation than the only other alternative they considered—that

Jesus was a prodigal. Had he turned into a degenerate because they had failed to raise him right?

When his mother and brothers found him after he left Nazareth, he was teaching in a house in Capernaum. What must they have been thinking as they came to the door (Mk 3:31–35)? There Mary was, come to help her *misguided* son, and Jesus was inside teaching, *guiding* if you will, those who eagerly listened and believed in him. What painful irony.

Inside the house, in the middle of teaching, someone told him his mother and brothers were at the door to see him. Jesus refused them—at least his statement could be interpreted as a refusal. He asked, "Who are my mother and my brothers?" (Mk 3:33, NIV). Of course, if Mary and the brothers heard him say that, they might have concluded for certain he was crazy and needed help. Or, perhaps they suspected an even more painful truth, that he was not crazy, but rather that his blood kin were no longer wanted or welcome.

√But could it be that Jesus was using humor again? If he knew they suspected he was crazy, and if he knew that they had come to take him away, then to say *Who are my mother and my brothers?* would be a playfully mocking thing to do. They might have thought for a moment, *Oh my, he really is delirious. He's lost his mind, unable to recognize even his own mother, the poor man.* But as is usually the case when Jesus shows his sense of humor, there is a very sane message behind it. In this case, he was making it clear that anyone who does the will of his heavenly Father has become family. Jesus's blood kin are no longer central to who he is or what he is doing. Perhaps in his own teasing way, he was telling them he's not crazy. He knew *exactly* what he was doing, and he had no intention of being restrained or put away.

It may seem a terrible thing Jesus did, putting off his family. But any counselor would confirm the significant degree to which unsevered ties to parents impede the lives of adults.

Grown children are leaving home later and later. Our culture fosters a continuing dependent relationship between adult children and their parents.

In our prevailing society, there are still remnants of ancient ceremonies of initiation into adulthood. Though less dramatic than those of ancient societies, they are very important. Circumcision. Bar mitzvah. Baptism. Confirmation. Spelling bees. Football. Chess tournaments. Tattooing. Hazings. Deer hunts. Bachelor parties. Graduations. Marriages and births. Ancient peoples marked such occasions with symbols, totems, and scarring. Today we mark them with certificates, trophies, and videotapes.

Unlike ancient peoples, the modern break with parents—if it happens at all—is often long and drawn out. True, some teens run away, or maybe join the army. But many young people live out extended childhoods in a kind of limbo between boy and man, girl and woman. Jesus, however, completed his departure from home quickly and cleanly. He came to have only one father, his heavenly Father, who was all he needed, and he said so, whether it hurt his parents' feelings or not. Even at age twelve, the age of initiation in most ancient cultures, Jesus declared his separation from his parents by staying behind in the temple, deep in dialogue with grown men, and by pronouncing the temple his home, and God as his Father (Lk 2:49). This was an intentional act of initiation.

At the outset of his ministry, at about age thirty, the age at which a man was first allowed to read the Scriptures in synagogue on Sabbath, Jesus made it clear that he had only one family: those who did the will of his heavenly Father. And he said so, whether his blood kin approved or not. "My mother and my brothers are those who hear the word of God and do it" (Lk 8:21, NRSV).

Are we offended by Jesus's brusqueness with his family of origin, his refusals of them, his "rejections" of them? If so, our offense is strong evidence of our problem: Our culture discourages young adults from separating cleanly from their parents and childhood. To break resolutely, one must refuse to remain a dependent. In short, to one's parents one must say No. When they appear at the door, one must ask, *Who are my mother and my brothers?* There should be little danger in doing this, except of course for the small problem of one's parents believing one to be a psychotic.

Unplug Your Mind: Over what does your family question your sanity?

Conclusion

Jesus said No to acquaintances, followers, foes, and family. Not all of the scriptural instances of Jesus saying No were uncovered in these first three chapters. Nor were the "No" instances covered here exhausted of their meaning. You should feel free to wring them out some more. But now is a good time to turn from the times Jesus said No to the times Jesus checked out.

4

|/ HE CHECKED OUT

"Everyone is searching for you."

—Mark 1:37b

Someone who "checked out" has simply gotten up and
left. Exited. Walked out. That is what Chapter 4 is about.
It is about those times when Jesus just got up and left. If
you are unaware of this checking out pattern in Jesus's ministry, this will be a revelation to you. If you are already aware
of this pattern, then you will enjoy remembering how, when,
where, and why Jesus chose to check out.

Jesus Leaves a Waiting Crowd

The story of Jesus leaving the house in Capernaum may be
the most overlooked story of Jesus's ministry. One reason it is
overlooked is that it is told explicitly only in Mark's Gospel,
and Mark is usually voted last in gospel popularity polling.
(Actually, this event is recorded in Luke 4:42–43 as well, but
there it is more of a transitional episode.) Another reason it is
overlooked may be that it seems at first glance simply insig-
nificant. However, at second glance it is a little troubling. At
third glance? Well, you be the judge.

In the first chapter of Mark, the very beginning of Jesus's
public ministry in Galilee (Mk 1:21–39), Jesus was teaching
in the Capernaum synagogue on the Sabbath, perhaps for the
first time. He healed someone in the synagogue that day—
and lo and behold—no one got mad. They actually seemed to
like it, unlike other times and places where devout Jews were

offended by Jesus healing on the Sabbath (Mt 12:10; Mk 2:24, 3:2; Lk 6:7, 13:14, 14:3; Jn 5:16, 7:23, 9:14–16). [**FYI:** Some Jews, perhaps most in that day, felt that the practice of medicine—which is how they classified the act of healing—was "work." And working on the Sabbath was forbidden.] But in Capernaum, they were apparently more flexible about such regulations, and had no problem with Jesus healing on the Lord's day (Mk 1:27).

After the worship service, Jesus and the disciples went to Peter and Andrew's house where Peter's mother-in-law was sick in bed. Jesus healed her, and there they spent the rest of the day. [**FYI:** Mark says Jesus made his home in Capernaum (Mk 2:1). It is impossible to say with certainty which specific house it was or where it was located, but many scholars assume they took their residence with Peter's mother-in-law. In the excavations of Capernaum is a house identified by some archaeologists as the very house where this story takes place.]

At sundown that same day, when the Sabbath was officially over, the people of Capernaum began showing up at this house with all their sick or insane friends and family members. Pretty soon, there in the dusk of a Saturday evening, practically the whole town was lined up at the door, and Jesus opened it to them. This went on all night. Sick people, crippled people, crazy people, hour after hour; the line did not seem to get any shorter.

Just before dawn, while it was still dark, without explanation or warning, *Jesus checked out!* He told no one that he was leaving, he told no one where he was going, and he told no one why. *He just left.* He walked to a deserted place all alone. Why? Was it rest he needed? Time to himself? We can speculate all we like. Mark says he went for one reason, and one reason only: prayer (Mk 1:35).

It was not long before word reached Peter. Jesus was missing. *Terrific.* The sick were lined up for miles. They had a blockbuster on their hands. Things were finally taking off, and in a big way. But the star was missing in action! Just great.

They had scoured the house and the immediate vicinity, to no avail. Peter got his buddies together and formed a Jesus search party. They lit some lamps, slipped out, and followed the trail up the hill and out of town. When they finally found Jesus, they all approached and said, "Everyone is searching for you" (Mk 1:37, RSV).

This is the only statement Mark records. Perhaps they said more. Perhaps there was a lengthy conversation. We cannot know. Yet implicit in that one sentence—*Everyone is searching for you*—is a world of meaning, not the least of which was their intent to bring him back to Capernaum for a curtain call.

Jesus's response to them is nothing short of shocking: *No, I'm not going back,* he said. *It's almost morning anyway, so let's go on to some different towns. This healing thing is part of the picture, but I've got a message to spread, and that's really why I went public* (based on Mk 1:38).

Another No to his disciples. This time, he walked away from a crowd of people waiting to be healed! Why? His ministry of teaching was a priority over a healing ministry, even though the healing was an immediate, giant success. Remarkable.

Yet the most remarkable aspect of this story, and the point of discussing it, is that Jesus made a habit of checking out. Luke puts it like this: "Many crowds would gather to hear him and to be cured of their diseases. But he would withdraw to deserted places and pray" (Lk 5:16, NRSV).

Jesus offered no explanation or apology, nor did he ask permission. He just went. And he did it again and again, leaving waiting crowds so that he could go pray by himself. In another chapter (6:12), Luke writes, "Now during those days he went out to the mountain to pray; and he spent the night in prayer to God" (NRSV).

To fail to take note of this pattern in the Gospels is to miss an essential clue as to who Jesus was, and, consequently, who Christians are called to be.

"Place the oxygen mask on yourself first, and then on children or others requiring assistance." Those who have flown a commercial airliner are familiar with this spiel. Most flyers pay no attention, but it is a beautiful parable of self-care. If you try to help others first, you might pass out, and then you might all suffocate. But if you secure your mask first, then you are fit to assist others. Jesus said essentially the same thing in Matthew 7:5: *You hypocrite! First take the log out of your own eye. Then you can see clearly to help your brother with the splinter in his.*

In other words, taking care of yourself is not selfish, but is absolutely necessary if you are to be of any use to God.

Jesus checked out as needed, and the moments he chose to leave are fascinating and instructive to anyone who would follow him.

Unplug Your Mind: Do you consider time alone to be an inconvenience that you can't fit in or an embarrassment that you make excuses for? Why or why not?

✓Jesus Has Three Reasons to Leave

Jesus had not planned to feed the 5,000 (Mt 14:13–21; Mk 6:30–44; Lk 9:10–17; Jn 6:1–15). On the contrary, being around people was the last thing he wanted. Jesus tried to escape by boat, but he did not count on all those people following along the coastline on foot. The exit plan failed. So what could he do but go ashore, show compassion, postpone the vacation time, and address the needs of those in front of him? Note: He did not *cancel* the checkout time, merely *postponed* it, and postponed it for as brief a time as possible.

The Gospels do not agree on Jesus's main reason for checking out on this occasion. There is Matthew's version and

Mark's version, and then Luke's seems to blend these. (John's is so radically different that it has to be handled separately.) Each explanation alone was reason enough to immediately call a travel agent. But when put together, well, anyone who kept working without a break under those circumstances deserved whatever ulcer, hemorrhoid, hive, or migraine he got!

The way Matthew tells it, Jesus had just heard that Herod Antipas had beheaded John the Baptist in prison (Mt 14:1–12). John's head had been paraded around a banquet hall on a silver platter! His disciples came and took the body and buried it. Then they traveled to Galilee to tell Jesus.

While the personal bond between Jesus and John the Baptist sometimes goes unnoticed, that is merely because the Gospel writers were dispelling notions of John's superiority to Jesus. John himself apparently had a lot of followers, many of whom thought *him* to be the messiah. To counter that mistake, our four Gospel writers are careful to subordinate John, and they mention precious little of the close relationship that John and Jesus had. We get hints of a relationship here and there, especially in the Gospel of John, but not much.

Yet, in this instance, Matthew is clear and unambiguous. Jesus hears of what Antipas did to John the Baptist. John's disciples themselves traveled all that way to break the news to Jesus personally. Matthew writes, "Now when Jesus heard this, he withdrew from there in a boat to a deserted place by himself. But when the crowds heard it, they followed him on foot from the towns. When he went ashore, he saw a great crowd; and he had compassion for them … " (Mt 14:13–14, RSV).

So, according to Matthew, at least two things drove Jesus to check out. First, his association with John made Antipas's territory for him a dangerous place. We learn later that Jesus's instincts, of course, were right—that Antipas was indeed looking for him: "But Herod said, 'I beheaded John. Who, then, is this I hear such things about?' And he tried to see him" (Lk 9:9, NIV).

Matthew

Then the second reason Jesus checked out is obvious: *grief*. He had suffered a great loss. John was gone. Jesus actually called him Elijah, equating John with Israel's greatest prophet: "' … but I tell you that Elijah has already come, and they did not recognize him, but they did to him whatever they pleased. So also the Son of Man is about to suffer at their hands.' Then the disciples understood that he was speaking to them about John the Baptist" (Mt 17:12–13, NRSV). Jesus also said, "Truly I tell you, among those born of women no one has arisen greater than John the Baptist … " (Mt 11:11, NRSV). John meant a lot to Jesus personally, there is little doubt. And we know that grief can be persistent, even merciless. If you do not pay attention to it, it will mess with you. It was dangerous for Jesus to be in Galilee at that point, and the time away was needed to grieve for John. This is Matthew's version.

In Mark, John's beheading is in the background, so that no specific connection is made between Jesus wanting time away and the Baptist's death. There is no mention of John's disciples coming to tell Jesus. Mark introduces another reason altogether for their sabbatical: He reminds us that the disciples had been out on a mission two by two, and that they had just returned (Mk 6:6b–13). They met with Jesus to give reports on all that they had said and done. Mark writes that, "The apostles gathered around Jesus, and told him all that they had done and taught. He said to them, 'Come away to a deserted place all by yourselves and rest a while.' For many were coming and going, and they had no leisure even to eat" (Mk 6:30–31, NRSV).

For Mark, neither grief for John nor worry about Antipas is the reason given for leaving. The only reason Mark gives is that Jesus senses that his disciples are tired and in need of rest. That's it.

In conclusion, there are three legitimate reasons to take an unplanned holiday:

1. You have been working very hard and you are tired.
2. Someone you love has died and you need time to grieve.
3. An evil ruler is trying to kill you!

The third of these obviously happens less often than the first two for most of us, unless we choose to read it metaphorically: *Evil forces are converging to sabotage your life or steal your work.*

That being the case, one would need time out to plan a strategy to combat such an attack. Resting, grieving, and strategizing are all legitimate reasons for checking out, then and today.

Unplug Your Mind: What signals tell you it's time to check out, and what will likely happen if you don't?

Jesus Sends Them All Away

As he tried to leave for Bethsaida, Jesus's vacation plans were postponed by the crowd following them on foot—but only postponed. Downtime was still next on the agenda. The 5,000 men, *plus* women and children (Mt 14:21), got fed. It was finally time to go. But Jesus handled this retreat very differently (Mk 6:45–47).

He did three things. First, he made the disciples get back in the boat and go on to the other side without him. He gave no reason why, and it is easy to imagine the disciples protesting. Second, he dismisses the crowd himself. Third, he goes up the mountain by himself to pray. Alone.

This new plan is very different from the first. Initially, they were meant to go for retreat together, Jesus and his disciples. The issues were three: fatigue, grief, and danger. A crowd-in-need interrupted Plan A. Yet we presume that once the crowd was gone, Jesus would try to implement Plan A again. Wrong.

This time Jesus did not want to be alone with his disciples. He wanted to be alone, period. Keep in mind he was already tired and griefstricken when the crowd came along. Instead of getting away, he ended up working all day. Now, instead of wanting to hang with his friends, he wanted to be completely alone. Was he mad at one of the disciples, was he feeling poorly? All we know is that he came up with Plan B: *You guys sail across without me; I'll send the crowd away, and I'm going up this mountainside somewhere to pray alone. I'll see you when I see you.*

As shocking as it may sound, Jesus was not on duty twenty-four hours a day. Sure, he worked some overtime hours, but there is no example in the Gospels of Jesus apologizing for punching out on the time clock. He paid close attention to himself, to his needs, and he did that because paying attention to God required it. It still does. Never, ever, under any circumstances apologize for breaks, recess, naps, leisure time, recreation, outings, vacations, trips, tours, sabbaticals, holidays, furloughs, liberty, or shore leave. By the way, the only antonym to all of these is "work."

Unplug Your Mind: How do you tell those closest to you that you need to be alone without feeling guilty or having to apologize?

Jesus Has a Fourth Reason to Leave

John's version of the feeding of the 5,000 (6:1–15) is what I like to call the Twilight Zone version: When the crowd had filled their stomachs with five loaves and two fish, it began to register to the masses what Jesus had done. They knew of his teaching and his healing, but this "sign" was something else altogether. They began to talk: "This is indeed the prophet who is to come into the world" (Jn 6:14, ESV).

In their enthusiasm, the people came up with a plan that Jesus wanted no part of:

Then Jesus, because he knew they were going to come and seize him by force to make him king, withdrew again up the mountainside alone (Jn 6:15, NET).

They were ready to make him king!

The irony of this is that you cannot make Jesus king. He is already king. Their coronation attempt only reveals their ignorance. They saw the multiplication of the loaves and fish, but they did not understand what it signified. They did not see that the bread was his body to be broken to feed the world. And his enthronement would not be accomplished by the will of a clueless Galilean fan club, but by the will of God on the tree at Golgotha (the Place of the Skull; the site of Jesus's execution). The crowd may have been speaking among themselves: *Can King Herod Antipas do the things this man can do? Antipas is nothing. He's a Roman lackey. God is with Jesus the Prophet, and we are with him! We're not afraid of any Roman now, for we will make him our king. No one can harm God's Anointed One. He will save us from the tyrants. Hail Jesus, the new King of Israel!*

John does not tell us how Jesus escaped, only that he did. He did quite a bit of escaping. He had to dodge the Jewish authorities, Herod, and thousands of excited Jews.

The Scriptures paint a simple but chilling picture that easily demonstrates Jesus's motives for checking out, again and again.

• **Mark 1:45**—Jesus could no longer enter a town openly but stayed outside in lonely places.

• **Luke 13:31**—At that time some Pharisees came to Jesus and said to him, "Leave this place and go somewhere else. Herod wants to kill you."

• **John 6:15**—Jesus, knowing that they intended to come and make him king by force, withdrew again to a mountain by himself.

• **John 11:8**—"But Rabbi," they said, "a short while ago the Jews there tried to stone you, and yet you are going back?"

• **John 11:54**—Therefore Jesus no longer moved about publicly among the Jews. Instead he withdrew to a region near the wilderness, to a village called Ephraim, where he stayed with his disciples (All verses from Today's New International Version).

Visibility became a liability. This is another reason Jesus became so determined and intentional about checking out.

Unplug Your Mind: Has there been a time when the enthusiasm and affirmation of your peers drove you to check out?

Jesus Leaves to Contemplate His Return

Jesus fled Galilee heading north. To escape the crowds? To get away from Antipas? To grieve John's death? To rest? All of the above? He traveled to Tyre and Sidon where he encountered the Syrophoenecian woman (see Chapter 1), and then he continued on to the territory of Herod Philip, Antipas's brother, and the city of Caesarea Philippi, the capital (Mt 16:13).

He certainly had more anonymity in that region, and he would not have been under the scrutiny of Antipas's spies. (Mk 3:6) But there was another reason for his retreat north, a darker and more terrifying reason than Peter and the others could have yet imagined. Jesus was about to openly discuss his destiny.

Jesus was again troubled and praying alone one day with only his disciples near him. What took place, Luke says, is to be understood in the context of Jesus's withdrawal to pray (Lk 9:18). Caesarea Philippi is sprawled before them, the ancient city of Panias with its magnificent Temple of Pan guarding a large cavern from which the headwaters of the Jordan river flowed. The Cave of Pan yawned before them, a place believed to be the portal to Hades itself. And death was on his mind.

When Jesus broke the silence, he said, "Who do people say that I am?" (Mk 8:29; see also Mt 16:13 and Lk 9:18, NET).

This came out of the blue. He had never asked anything like that before. Where was he going with this? They answered him based on what they had overheard people saying. Most people felt that Jesus was a great prophet returned from the dead. Some were saying John the Baptist, some Elijah, Jeremiah, and various others.

Was Jesus doubting himself? Who was he, and what was God calling him to do next? Is that why he asked them what others thought of him? And why would he care?

Of course we cannot know what Jesus was thinking, but he and the disciples were holed up in a foreign territory doing little more than hiding out, and Jesus was more and more alone and in prayer. It was obvious that something was brewing. *Who do people say that I am?* What answer was he hoping for? Did he really expect the people in the crowds to understand who he was and what he was doing? Was he himself pondering at this point where his mission was, and where it was heading? A strange question—*Who do people say that I am?*—and yet Jesus had another: "But who do *you* say that I am?" (Mt 16:15; Mk 8:29; Lk 9:20, NET [italics mine]).

One disciple answered this question according to scriptural record, and we have no way of knowing the tone of his answer. Did Peter respond timidly? Boldly? Did he mean it? Or was it merely what he thought Jesus wanted to hear?

"You are the Messiah," Mark 8:29b records him saying.

"The Messiah of God," Peter says in Luke 9:20b.

"You are the Messiah, the Son of the living God," he says in Matthew 16:16.

Only Matthew recounts Jesus blessing Peter for his answer, but all three Gospels have Jesus sternly warning them to tell no one that he is the Messiah. *You must tell no one! This is not the time for proclamation, for you do not yet understand what you are saying. Now listen to me. This is what I'm planning to do. I'm planning to go to Jerusalem, and Jerusalem will not accept my message or me. The leaders of the people will arrest and torture me. They will hand me over to the Romans who will execute me as a criminal. And on the third day I will rise* (based on Mt 16:21; Mk 8:31; Lk 9:21-22).

Well, this didn't seem like such a great plan to the disciples. Peter grabbed Jesus and yelled at him. Jesus turned his back on Peter and rebuked him, calling him "Satan," and accusing him of not being on the side of God (Mt 16:22–23; Mk 8:32–33).

I imagine on that evening no one commented on what a nice day it had been.

And think, it all began with Jesus alone in prayer. Who would have thought prayer could cause such a mess?

Unplug Your Mind: How can prayer lead to confrontation?

Jesus Leaves to Converse with Moses and Elijah

Jesus and his disciples were still in Caesarea Philippi six days later (Mt 17:1–9; Mk 9:2–10). *Six days later.* That must have been a hellish week. Disagreements. Long silences. Constant prayer. Jesus had told them he was going to Jerusalem, but six sunrises had come and gone. Was he hesitating? Rethinking? Searching for courage? Preparing himself? The Gospels do not say.

But on that sixth day he took Peter, James, and John up the slopes of Mount Hermon, a great mountain directly above the city—a windblown, barren slope high enough to be mantled with snow during the cold months, shrouded in winter mists and layer upon layer of drifting, ghostly fog.

At the summit, there was that deafening silence one hears in the wilderness. It was just the four of them surveying the world below. Not a word was spoken. Jesus stood apart from them, and without warning, the Gospels agree, he took on an unearthly appearance. The three disciples saw him in his eternal glory transcending time and space. For the first time they knew for sure that they were in the presence of a mystery and a power that they could not fathom.

Moreover, Moses and Elijah appeared, and they by their appearance were also not bound by time and space as we understand them, and they began to speak with Jesus. The three disciples heard the three radiant ones speaking of Jesus's departure, and the things he must accomplish in Jerusalem.

Get this: The prophet of God who faced down the Pharaoh of Egypt (Ex 5–12), and the prophet of God who faced down the Prophets of Baal (1 Kgs 18), spoke to Jesus of his facing down the religious leaders of Jerusalem! The man of Mt. Sinai and the man of Mt. Carmel encouraged the man who would ascend Mt. Zion (on which Jerusalem was built). It was a conference of mountain men!

You're on the right track, Jesus. Don't back down.

The conversation continued into the night, and poor Peter, James, and John were exhausted. Though they were weighted down with sleep, they managed to stay awake.

Then Moses and Elijah turned to leave. Peter jumped up.

Master we can build some shelters for you and for them, so they can stay the night. We may not be good for much, but we should do something.

But while Peter was speaking, a heavy mist rolled in. They grew disoriented and terrified as they entered the dense cloud. And from the darkness a voice spoke to them as clear and as plain as a human voice.

Jesus is my Son. I have chosen him. Start listening to him (based on Mk 9:7).

They stumbled around in the blackness until they found Jesus. He was alone and silent. They spent the night huddled together without much to say. When they descended the mountain with Jesus the next morning, none of them said anything to the others about what had happened. They could barely believe it themselves.

As for the outcome of the meeting, Luke says it best:

" … as the time drew near for him to be taken up, he resolutely turned his face towards Jerusalem" (Lk 9:51, NJB).

It was time to meet his destiny.

"'The Son of Man is going to be delivered into the hands of men, and they will kill him. And when he is killed, after three days he will rise.' But they did not understand the saying, and were afraid to ask him" (Mk 9:31–32, ESV).

What the disciples were thinking at this point is hard to say. Events of the next few weeks suggest they still did not understand who Jesus was and why he was going to Jerusalem. They were exceedingly anxious. All four Gospels make that clear.

As Mark puts it: *They were on the road going up to Jerusalem, and Jesus was striding ahead of them, and everyone behind him was amazed and afraid* (based on Mk 10:32).

The time on the mountain in prayer, with Peter, James, and John nearby, and Moses and Elijah there to affirm and encourage him, had steeled his nerve. Understandably, Jesus had struggled, even hesitated there at Caesarea Philippi. But not even the hounds of hell could stop him now.

Unplug Your Mind: How has God prepared you to meet your destiny, that is, go to your Jerusalem?

Jesus Asks His Father for an Alternative

On the way to Jerusalem, the Gospel writers recorded no other instances of Jesus slipping away. There was no checking out now that Jesus was on the final leg of the journey. He had one purpose and one destination. No withdrawal, retreat, or leave time required.

Yet, at the very end, in Gethsemane, Jesus withdrew one last time from the disciples, at a distance of about a stone's throw, and he knelt down, and prayed. "Abba, Father, all things are possible for you. Remove this cup from me. Yet not what I will, but what you will" (Mk 14:32; Mt 26:39, Lk 22:42, ESV).

He went back, and the disciples were sleeping through their grief. After scolding them for falling asleep, he went away to pray again, throwing himself on the ground and asking God if there might be another way. Three times he did this. The struggle was so intense that it threatened to crush him. Some ancient copies of Luke record that Jesus was in such anguish as he prayed that his sweat became like great drops of blood falling to the ground (Lk 22:44). [**FYI:** Ironically, the word Gethsemane means *oil press*. Olive squeezings provided oil for cooking, for lamps, and for soap. There were three separate, consecutive squeezings for these.] Three times Jesus prayed for relief as he was squeezed by the pressure of impending events in a place called the Oil Press. [**FYI:** Medically, blood can mix with sweat in rare and extreme cases of "pressure." What greater pressure can you imagine than the pressure Jesus faced in deciding to face his arrest, torture, and execution?[1]]

In Chapter 9, *He Called Believers to Stand, Follow, and Divide*, we will return to Gethsemane. But for now, what must be highlighted is his act of withdrawing for prayer, especially in that grove of olive trees on the side of the Mount of Olives.

Perhaps it is true of all of Jesus's prayer times apart, but especially in Gethsemane, that there is the distinct flavor of a face-off. His prayers never took on the tone of an emptying, karma, in-tune-ness, at-one-with-the-universe, at-peace-with-myself exercise. The impression is that his prayers were conversational struggles, more of a dialogue on issues than a mystical meditation. There was a vigorousness, a vocal exchange, almost an ongoing debate. Jesus talked things out with the Father. Very self-ish of him, indeed, to question the will of God for his life.

Unplug Your Mind: Jesus struggled with decisions and asked God to change his mind. Do you think you have the right to do the same?

Conclusion

Jesus separated himself for prayer so often, and yet few ask, Why? Was he hoping God would tell him what to do, fix his problems, give him courage, or charge his batteries? What was he doing, and what was happening when he prayed?

Yes, he checked out when he was tired, when he was grieving, when he was under pressure, when he was struggling with decisions, and—in the end—when he had to face death. Yes, slipping away for prayer was not a habit, nor was it a compulsion for Jesus; it was standard operating procedure.

Certainly prayer was essential to Jesus's life and work. And the heart of his prayer was his intimate relationship to his Father. Jesus called God "Abba," which means Daddy, an unusually casual address, and some might even say an irreverent one. The Judean Fun Patrol did not even like it when he called God "Father" (pater—a common title for a male parent), much less "Daddy" (abba—a child's name for his father): "For this reason the Jews tried all the harder to kill him; not only was he breaking the Sabbath, but he was even calling God his own Father (pater), making himself equal with God" (Jn 5:18, NIV).

But the familiarity of this language witnesses to his closeness to God and how often they talked. Jesus checked out and talked to "Daddy" even when it created tension with those around him, and even when they complained about it as an inconvenience or interruption.

Jesus could live with being disappointing and confusing to people, even those closest to him, but he could not go on without checking out regularly and unapologetically.

Dr. Baxter Kruger and I were discussing this chapter, and he asked me, "How did Jesus survive the accusations and attacks? He stood up in the truth of who he was in the face of constant hate and harassment. I mean, they tore him down *every day*. How do you endure that?" It was a rhetorical question. Baxter knows how, and I know how, and after reading this chapter so do you. How else could he have done it? It was by checking out for prayer.

5

HE DISTURBED THE PEACE

*"As a lion or a young lion growls over its prey,
and—when a band of shepherds is called out against
it—is not terrified by their shouting or daunted at their
noise, so the Lord of hosts will come down to fight
upon Mount Zion and upon its hill."*

—Isaiah 31:4

Jesus is the lion. The pesky complaints of critics and officials, even friends and disciples, do not deter him. He growls over his prey, tears at it, and has no fear that anything can drive him from his kill. He is merciless in his determination to take his hill. He is relentless. Dauntless.

What were their complaints against Jesus? The accusations against him were somehow both serious and silly. Take Sabbath-breaking for instance. The fourth commandment given to Moses on Mt. Sinai concerned the Sabbath:

> "Remember the sabbath day, and keep it holy. Six days you shall labor and do all your work. But the seventh day is a sabbath to the Lord your God; you shall not do any work—you, your son or your daughter, your male or female slave, your livestock, or the alien resident in your towns. For in six days the Lord made heaven and earth, the sea, and all that is in them, but rested the seventh day; therefore the Lord blessed the sabbath day and consecrated it" (Ex 20:8–11, NRSV).

To accuse Jesus of Sabbath-breaking was a serious charge in the sense that he was being accused of breaking one of the Ten Commandments. Yet it was a silly charge as well, because the "violation" of which he was accused was healing sick people (The practice of medicine was considered "work," and you were not supposed to work on the Sabbath.) For healing people on a Saturday, Jesus was a sinner? A lawbreaker? A profaner of the Lord's Day? A transgressor of the Ten Commandments? A violator of the Law of Moses?

And there were other accusations equally serious and silly: hand-washing violations, the blasphemy of forgiving sins, failure to fast, and making disciples of known sinners. Silly or not, however, Jesus did not respond softly and tenderly. The Lion of Judah has teeth.

So Much for Shabbat Shalom (Sabbath Peace)

Jesus stood in the synagogue, righteous rage burning within him (Mk 3:1–6). He is in a hostile synagogue in an unnamed Galilean village. This is early in his ministry. And this is the only place in Scripture where it comes right out and says he is spitting mad. "He looked around at them with anger" (Mk 3:5a, NRSV).

He faced his detractors in the synagogue and leveled his gaze on them one by one as he panned across the congregation. These people were despicable. Their hardness of heart made him sick. He was about to cure some poor crippled man, and these jackals and hyenas were skulking around, lying in wait to accuse him of breaking a Sabbath law. Forget healing and health. To hell with hope and happiness for this unfortunate fellow, because they might violate one of their precious regulations! The effrontery. The incivility. The cruelty. It was absolutely abhorrent to him.

He devoured them with his eyes as he spoke: *Is it against the law to do good on the Sabbath, or would you prefer I do harm?*

*How about saving a life on the Sabbath, or maybe you would prefer
I kill?* (based on Mk 3:4).

But they were silent. It was as quiet as a church!

Matthew records this additional saying by Jesus on this
occasion:

Just imagine for a second that you only own one sheep, he said.
*One is all you have. What if it fell in a pit on the Sabbath. What
would you do? You know perfectly well what you would do! You'd go
down there, lay hold of it, and haul it out. Now think! Is a human
being less valuable than a sheep?* (based on Mt 12:11–12).

More silence.

"Stretch out your hand," Jesus told the injured man (Mk
3:5b).

The man did. And his withered hand was restored. The
congregation was furious. Pharisees bolted for the door to
report to Herod's spies. Already, even early in Jesus's ministry,
the leaders were conspiring with the Romans. Herod's people
were paranoid about rebels and insurrectionists. The religious
leaders hoped to use that to their advantage. To kill him.

Kill him?

Stone him?

Destroy him?

What had Jesus done to deserve such hatred, (Jn 7:7, 15:18,
24, 25) such hostility? (Lk 11:53) He went around teaching.
So what? He healed some sick people. So what? Do these
merit the religious leaders' contempt, their determination to
literally take him out? That is an awful lot of trouble to go
to over a traveling preacher. *If you don't like what the revival
preacher says, just don't invite him back next year!* Why hate him?
Why hate him so much that you want him dead?

But, that was not it. It was not so much what he *said* or
what he *did* that made them hate him. It was what he was.

He was a lion—fearless, strong, and dangerous. It was his
nature they feared. His heart. His mettle. His power. Gone
is my image of a fragile, retiring sage. We are talking about a

prowling, sinewy predator. You just cannot let a lion run loose. Especially not if you are a jackal or a hyena!

One Sabbath Jesus and the disciples were traveling through a wheat field (Mk 2:23-28). Some of them plucked heads off, rubbed them in their hands, and ate. The fun patrol—some Pharisees—popped up like scarecrows to challenge them for "working" on the Sabbath. [**FYI:** Harvesting was considered work, and therefore illegal on the Lord's Day—Friday sunset to Saturday sunset.] Jesus said, *You guys don't read your Scriptures, do you? Don't you remember when David was hungry, and he went into the temple, he ate the bread of the Presence, and shared it with his friends? The Sabbath was made for man, not man for the Sabbath. Besides, the Son of Man is Lord of the Sabbath. Go home, read your Scriptures, and quit hanging out in wheat fields!* (based on Mk 2:25–28).

He taught in another synagogue (Lk 13:10–17). It was the same song, second verse. There was a woman there who had been crippled for eighteen years, and he healed her. When he did, the leader of that synagogue announced to his congregation that there are six whole days a week you can go to the doctor, but one day a week that the doctor should not work. (Lk 13:14)

Jesus shot back, *You fakers! You frauds! You'll untie your precious jackass from the manger for a drink of water on the Sabbath, but this woman, this daughter of Abraham, tied up by Satan for eighteen long years, has to stay tethered until tomorrow? Go ahead and say it to her face: "Sorry, ma'am. Regulations." You bunch of ignorant hypocrites!* (based on Lk 13:15–16)

A Jewish man had been paralyzed for thirty-eight years (Jn 5:2–18). Jesus found him in a pagan temple dedicated to a god called Serapis, or Asclepias.[1] The god's symbol was a staff with a snake entwining it. Snakes played an important role in ancient pagan healing ritual and medical practice, and Asclepius's snake-entwined staff is familiar today as the caduceus, the symbol of modern medicine. It is believed that each morning a priest threw a snake in a pool, and it was believed that whoever got in the water first would be healed. Some later copies of John's Gospel include a verse 4 in Chapter 5, giving the explanation that *an angel* disturbed the water:

> "for an angel of the Lord went down at certain seasons into the pool, and stirred up the water; whoever then first, after the stirring up of the water, stepped in was made well from whatever disease with which he was afflicted" (Jn 5:4, NASB).

[**FYI:** The most ancient and reliable copies of John lack this verse (4). Most translations of the Bible place John 5:4 as a footnote because it is absent from the earliest copies of John that we have, and scholars believe it to be a gloss—words added by a later writer explaining, in this case, what might have stirred the water.[2] Archaeology has identified the five porticos of the Pool of Bethesda as an Asclepium—a pagan therapeutic center. These were located throughout the Roman world. Jerusalem's was located outside the north city wall and next to the Roman barracks called the Antonia Fortress. John records precisely where it was—by the Sheep Gate (Jn 5:2). So the Bethesda Pool was located between the Sheep Gate and the Antonia Fortress. Officers and soldiers and other pagan visitors are thought to have used the Asclepium as a sort of spa hospital.[3]

But if the Pool of Bethesda was a pagan temple, what is a crippled Jew doing there for thirty-eight years? That's probably what Jesus wanted to know. And did Jesus care that his own reputation and purity were tainted by entering a pagan worship area? Not a bit. He went there because at least one desperate person needed him.

Man, do you really want to be healed? Jesus asked him. The man whined about no one being there to get him in the pool fast enough to be first. *Stand up right now, take your mat, and get out of here!* Jesus ordered (based on Jn 5:6–8). And the man did. One problem: It was the Sabbath, and when the man entered the city, people began to harass him for toting his mat on the Lord's Day! He tried to reason with them, but he could not explain what had happened (without incriminating himself for being at a pagan temple!), and he said he did not know who had healed him or how (which was true) (Jn 5:13).

Later, Jesus saw the man in the temple and introduced himself. Then the man went and told the Judeans who it was that made him well, so they began to harass Jesus. His reply? "My Father is still working [on the Sabbath], and I also am working." The leaders were filled with malice, and they wanted him dead (Jn 5:17–18, NRSV).

✓It was the Sabbath again, and Jesus restored the sight to a blind man (Jn 9). *How can this Nazarene be of God when he has a blatant disregard for the Sabbath?* They interrogated the man to try and gather more evidence against Jesus. They hauled in his family as well, thinking maybe the whole thing was a hoax. The family was terrified. It had been rumored that anyone associated with Jesus might be put out of their synagogue. The parents confirmed that their son had been born blind, but that was all they knew.

Meanwhile, the former blind man grew more and more exasperated with the scholars' questions. He got up his nerve and challenged them: *This is unbelievable. You can't figure out whether Jesus is from God, but he opened my eyes! Never in the history of the world has somebody cured a man born blind. If he wasn't from God, he could do nothing, don't you see? Can't you people see?* (based on Jn 9:30–33).

To the man they said, "You were born entirely in sins, and you are trying to teach us?" (Jn 9:34, NRSV). And they bounced him out!

Later, when Jesus heard what had happened, he went and found the man. He told him who he was, and the man believed in him. Jesus said to him, *I came into this world to create a crisis, so that people who are blind can see, and people who see will go blind.* Some Pharisees spying nearby mocked, *Certainly you don't mean us, do you?* Jesus turned to them: *If you were blind, you would have no sin. But in saying, 'We see,' your sin remains* (based on Jn 9:39–41).

Jesus's problem with the Pharisees was their presumption of innocence. He meant that if you say, *I'm not a sinner,* the consequence is that you are exposing the truth about yourself—that you are blind to your own sin. That is why those who say *"We see"* cling to their sins rather than realizing that God forgives them. But when you know you are blind, and you know you are a sinner, then you are in a position to see and recognize and receive grace. And, as Jesus said to Simon the Pharisee, "But he who has been forgiven little loves little" (Lk 7:47, NIV).

Why would Jesus keep breaking the Sabbath law over and over? His enemies probably had their ideas: *He's ignorant and can't help it? He's sick and needs help? He's seeking attention? He's a nut? He's a troublemaker? He's anti-Jewish? He's showing off for his delinquent buddies? Disturbing the peace is his idea of fun? He's got a death wish? He's trying to be some sort of martyr for some obscure, extremist cause?*

It created such a stir, you would think Jesus would stop doing controversial stuff on the Sabbath, just to avoid the hassle. Maybe there was nothing really wrong with healing on the Sabbath, plucking grain on the Sabbath, or whatever. Granted. And yes, maybe he was right. Maybe the nitpicky traditions were stupid. But why flaunt them and create a disturbance? Why rile people up when it could so easily be avoided? Why irk people over and over when it was unnecessary? Was it really so important an issue, seeing as Jesus and the disciples had such a crucial message to deliver, so much good yet to do? What a shame to let hardheadedness about one little law jeopardize the whole mission, right? *Back off on this Jesus, for*

God's sake. You have to choose your battles. Is this the battlefield you want to die on?

Jesus obviously did not see it that way. Systematically and repeatedly, he challenged the hypocrisy of the Sabbath laws, as though he saw them as primary obstacles to his message and mission. He took them head on and never flinched. They were to him roadblocks to be crashed, and when he did it, he put the pedal to the metal. He rolled right into the synagogues, knowing he would offend them if he healed somebody, and he'd do it anyway. Jesus not only went after Sabbath laws, but other laws as well.

Unplug Your Mind: What should your pastor not be allowed to do on Sunday afternoon?

Clean Food and Clean Hands
Cannot Cleanse the Heart

The Pharisees once asked Jesus, *Why do your disciples break the ancient traditions, eating with defiled hands? Why don't they wash?* (based on Mk 7:1–23; Col 2:8, 20–23, 1 Pt 1:18).

They should have been wearing seatbelts.

Jesus shot back, *Isaiah was on the money about you fakers. He wrote, "These people glorify me, but it's only lip service. Their hearts have gone far from me; they worship in futility, teaching human ideas as theology." You hypocrites have abandoned the commandment of God to cling to your human traditions* (based on Mk 7:6–9).

But he was not done.

I'll give you an example. You know God said to honor your father and your mother. But you love your little loopholes more, don't you. You can give the pension set aside for your parents to the temple without breaking your tradition. Your parents become destitute, but that's OK because it's legal according to the your traditions, and you look oh-so-generous before others giving all that extra cash 'to God!' Ha! For the sake of your manmade regulations you make God's words null and void. And you do lots of things like that (based on Mk 7:10–13).

Jesus called together the crowd, still fired up.

Come! Gather around. Listen to me, all of you. Listen and understand: It is not what you put into your mouth that defiles you, but what comes out! Listen and understand. There is nothing outside of you that by going in can defile, but the things that come out are what defile! (based on Mk 7:14–15).

After the Pharisees had been thoroughly thrashed and the crowds had gone away, the disciples asked him privately, *What did you mean about nothing you put in your mouth can defile you?* (based on Mk 7:17).

Now Jesus was frustrated: *You fail to understand even this? Don't you see that food can't defile you? It goes in your mouth, down to your stomach, and eventually into the sewer. But what comes out of your mouth comes from within the human heart where all evil intentions come from. Need I list them for you? Everything from envy to murder. All of these things come from within, and they will most certainly defile you!* (based on Mk 7:18–23).

Unplug Your Mind: If external sources cannot defile, and all defilement orginates internally, then on what grounds are any foods or drinks prohibited?

He Used Healing to Prove He Could Forgive

He had come home to Capernaum, and the place was packed (Mk 2:1–12). Some people desperate for Jesus's attention pulled apart a section of the roof to lower their paralyzed friend down to him. When he saw their faith, he exclaimed, "My son, your sins are forgiven" (Mk 2:5, ESV).

Some scholars were hanging around as usual, and as usual they were offended.

How can he say that? It's blasphemy. Only God forgives sins! (based on Mk 2:6–7).

Jesus turned on them. *Why are you questioning this? You think forgiving sins is tough? Wait till you see this! 'Stand up and take your mat and walk.'* (based on Mk 2:8–9).

And the man got up and walked home.

If you cannot heal people, and I can, who are you *to question whether or not I can forgive sins? Which do you think is easier, healing a paralyzed man or forgiving a man's sins? You see that the man is healed. Now know this: The Son of Man has authority on earth to forgive sin, too. You can take that to the bank* (based on Mk 2:10–11).

They were dumbfounded.

Unplug Your Mind: What's the best way to question those who question you?

In Jesus You Are Seeing Something New

Still early in Jesus's ministry—Mark gives no location except that they are still somewhere in Galilee—some Pharisees complained: *We're fasting. Our disciples are fasting. John [the Baptist] and his disciples are fasting. Why don't your disciples fast?* (based on Mk 2:18).

Those Pharisees never seemed to tire of being beaten and humiliated.

Fast! Jesus exclaimed. *At a party? No way! Can the wedding guests fast while they are partying with the groom? Who on earth fasts while the groom is feasting and dancing? That would be crazy! But when the bridegroom is whisked away from them, then they will fast on that day.*

As usual, those without ears couldn't hear the words behind Jesus's celebration metaphor.

You don't get it do you? You are seeing something brand spanking new! Something that won't fit with the way things were before. You can't sew a piece of unshrunk cloth on an old coat, or the patch will pull away from it, the old from the new, and the tear is made worse.

You can't put new wine into old wineskins; it will burst the skins and the wine will leak on the ground, the skins torn beyond repair. You have to put new wine into new wineskins. So, fast if you want to, but you're missing the celebration of all time! (based on Mk 2:19–22).

Unplug Your Mind: Has anyone ever monitored you to the point of harassment? Has anyone *healthy* and *sane* ever monitored you to the point of harassment?

Jesus Picked Rejects for Disciples and Friends

Jesus saw Levi, son of Alphaeus, sitting at the tax booth on the road to Capernaum (Mk 2:13–17). He said to Levi, *If you want to be my disciple, leave your stuff. Let's go, right now.* And then Levi got up and followed Jesus. Filling one of his cabinet posts with a tax collector, a known traitor and thief, didn't exactly go over big with the highbrows.

As Jesus and his disciples walked along, Levi invited them all to his house for a banquet. Lots of tax collectors and other rejects were invited, too. The fun police were on alert again. Pharisees and scribes asked among themselves, "Why does he eat with tax collectors and sinners?" (Mk 2:16, ESV).

Hey, Jesus called to them, *do any of you call the doctor when nobody is sick?*

What? they asked.

I said, Do any of you call the doctor when nobody is sick? No? Then you should understand that I'm here for sinners, not the righteous, if anyone righteous truly exists (see Rom 3:10). *So if you never sin, go on home. We're trying to have a nice "sinner dinner" here!* (based on Mk 2:17).

Zacchaeus was a chief tax collector (Lk 19:1–10). He lived in palatial Jericho, and he got a cut from all the tax collectors under him. We know two things about Zacchaeus; One, he had no cash flow problems. And two—how can we put this delicately?—He was elevation deficient? Altitude constricted? Vertically challenged? OK, he was short (Lk 19:3).

Everyone complained when Jesus told the chief tax collector to get down out of the tree and take him to his house to eat. Grumble, grumble: *He has gone to be the guest of one who is a sinner.* Jesus did not care what they thought. As he walked away with Zacchaeus, he said to them, *I came to seek and save the lost. If you're not lost, then get lost, and leave us to eat our lunch in peace* (based on Lk 19:10).

The longest conversation recorded in Scripture between Jesus and another individual is his talk with the Samaritan woman at Jacob's well (Jn 4:1–42). He should not have been in Samaria at all. The fun police really frowned on that. But he traveled through Samaria anyway, almost rubbing his proximity to Samaritans in their faces. [**FYI:** He told an outrageous parable about a "good" Samaritan (Lk 10:25–37). And he healed a Samaritan leper who came back to thank him (Lk 17:11–19). The fun police even began to accuse him of *being* a Samaritan (Jn 8:48).]

So there he was in Samaria. Again. The woman came to the well in the middle of the day. He should not have talked to a woman in public, especially a Samaritan woman. Even the disciples, when they returned from getting food, were so astonished they were afraid to ask him what in the *world* he thought he was doing—Jesus, alone with a woman of the hated Samaritans, at a well (Jn 4:27). [**FYI:** Old Testament wells were a good place to look for a wife! See Genesis 24, Genesis 29, and Exodus 2. Today, a different kind of watering hole tends to serve the same purpose!]

At the well Jesus was talking and sharing water with the woman, which must have reminded the disciples of the stories in Scripture where great lovers met at wells. To them it looked really bad. Spin-doctors went on high alert. They had their own reputations—and his—to maintain.

Never underestimate the power of reputation maintenance. For the disciples, how things looked to others mattered. What others thought and said mattered. It still matters, a whole lot, if the truth be told. Reputation is a driving force in everyday life. Especially for Christians! We are all image conscious, and not just of our personal image, but also of our family image, church image, community image, and national image. Who among us remembers *ever* doing the right thing, even when it looked really bad? That is the power of reputation.

A United Methodist church was considering canceling its Sunday evening services. The church was mostly in favor of this, as was the pastor, due to lack of interest and participation. (For shame, for shame!) When word got around about this, a vocal minority in the church made enough noise to raise Cain from the dead. Strangely, the voices opposed to the idea never attended Sunday evening services themselves!

The pastor was surprised at the energy behind the opposition and curious about why it was so important to them. What could be driving this? The vocal opponents did not even attend Sunday evening worship. Why should they care whether it was canceled?

After a little research, the pastor discovered that the concern was not for the loss of a weekly worship opportunity, but what the neighboring Baptist congregation would think of them for canceling it! Behold the power of reputation.

So the pastor made a subversive, playful, devious, wonderful, Jesus-like proposal at the next administrative board meeting. He proposed that they cancel Sunday evening services, but that everyone should drive to the church Sunday evening, and park their cars in the church lot so that it would *appear* that they were worshiping. Then everyone could walk over to Shoney's or to a movie or to the mall for an hour or two, come back for their cars, and drive home. That way when the Baptists drove by, it would *look* like people were there for worship!

They did not appreciate the pastor's "humor." But the church went ahead and canceled Sunday evening worship, with the stipulation that small group meetings would be moved to Sunday night, and the sanctuary would remain open Sunday for prayer. So the service was canceled, but action was taken nevertheless to make sure that cars would continue to be displayed Sunday evenings for the passing Baptists. *Never* underestimate the power of reputation.

The irony is that while Christians have a big thing about image, propriety, and respectability, Jesus was downright reckless in terms of who he hung out with, what he did, and when and where he did it. So reckless was Jesus that he had a reputation for being a glutton and a drunkard (Lk 7:34; Mt 11:19), a Samaritan (Jn 8:48), a friend of rejects and traitors (Lk 7:34; Mt 11:19), a lawbreaker and a sinner (Jn 9:24), and even possessed by demons (Jn 7:20, 8:48, 8:52, 10:20). That was our Lord's reputation! And yet he did not ever once express concern about his image. He could not have cared less. To him there was no contest: When he had to choose between doing right and looking respectable, he chose doing right. The Samaritan woman at Jacob's well could attest to that; he treated her with the utmost respect and friendship even though there were regulations forbidding such an encounter. Levi and Zacchaeus were treated with respect and friendship, regardless of regulations against associating with them. And the same goes for everyone he ever healed on the Sabbath; healing them was the right thing to do, even though manmade regulations blinded some to that fact.

Unplug Your Mind: What relationships do you hide to protect your reputation?

Conclusion

Jesus disturbed the peace: profoundly, repeatedly, and intentionally. While this conclusion might fly in the face of what we were taught in the past about Jesus, it is nonetheless true. He acted and spoke in ways that upset the apple cart, and occasionally he *nuked* the apple cart. He would not be turned away or intimidated by anyone, not by his mother, his brothers, his kin, his hometown, his disciples, his friends, his enemies, or even Satan. Here is the epigraph from the beginning of this chapter:

> "As a lion or a young lion growls over its prey, and—when a band of shepherds is called out against it—is not terrified by their shouting or daunted at their noise, so the Lord of hosts will come down to fight upon Mount Zion and upon its hill" (Is 31:4, RSV).

To those who challenged his behavior he was neither soft nor sweet. He cut them off at the knees. Those who dared to contest his habits were not spared his wrath. The Lion of Judah could not be driven from his kill.

Jesus ran roughshod over Sabbath regulations. He did not observe the traditions of the elders regarding washing, food, or fasting. He forgave sins to the shock of his learned opponents. And he picked rejects for disciples and friends. These practices ruined his reputation in the sight of some, and yet to others these were the very practices that brought him adoration, devotion, and praise.

It should be clear now that the Lion has come to Zion to feed. For those who are uncertain of their biblical geography, Mount Zion *is* Jerusalem. That was Jesus's destination and his destiny, and that will be the focus of the closing chapters of this book.

6

HE CORRECTED, CASTIGATED, AND DETONATED

"I reprove and discipline those whom I love."
—Revelation 3:19

As accepting and open as Jesus was to sinners and tax collectors, and as tender as he was with women and children, he was not a one-dimensional person. The Jesus of Scripture was more than kind and gentle. He was also a warrior who was unafraid of confrontation. When called for, he corrected, he castigated, and he detonated. And he did not reserve his sharp words for just his opponents. Disciples and friends were not spared.

Sometimes You Have to Correct Someone

One of the ways we sometimes keep the peace is to just let things go. *Don't make a scene. Don't make waves. Don't rock the boat. Don't stir things up.* Yet Jesus was quick to reject that philosophy. He corrected people, especially those closest to him. (I guess we all can be the most harsh with the people closest to us.) There is no doubt that it caused friction, but Jesus did it anyway. He must have had a high tolerance for conflict and tension. He lived in it constantly, and he often initiated it! It is amazing that his followers continued to love and support him considering the ever-present possibility of a stinging correction. It might have been some comfort had they had at their disposal the Book of Revelation (written decades after the crucifixion). After raking the church at Laodicea over the coals, the Lord said, "I reprove and discipline those whom I love" (Rv 3:19).

Perhaps that would have been some consolation to the many targets of Jesus's disapproval.

In Luke 10, Martha accused Jesus of not caring that Mary was sitting at his feet refusing to help around the house (38–42).

Martha, Martha, Jesus said, *you're so tense. How many number-one priorities is it possible for one woman to implement at the same time? Mary has picked one thing, and it's the best thing. There is no way I'm sending her away. I'll allow no one to take her from me, not even you* (based on Lk 10:41–42).

The very same Mary of Bethany poured an entire jar of expensive ointment on Jesus's feet and wiped them with her hair. (Jn 12:1–8). At seeing this, Judas Iscariot protested. *What a waste!* he said. *It could have been sold and the money given to the poor.*

Jesus commanded: *Be quiet and leave this woman alone. This is a beautiful thing she has done for me. She will be remembered forever for this, because by pouring this on my body, she has anointed me for burial. You can help the poor 365 days a year, but I don't have much time left. Leave her be* (based on Jn 12:7–8).

James and John, the so-called Sons of Thunder (Mk 3:17), were harassing a poor fellow who was healing people in Jesus's name (Mk 9:38–41). They tried to stop him because they had never seen him before, and he was not traveling with them "officially." When Jesus realized the disciples were interfering with the healer on his behalf, he chided them, saying, *Why did you try to stop him? If he's doing good in my name, he's certainly not going to turn around and speak evil of me. Let the man keep doing what he's doing, and don't bother him. Whoever isn't against us is for us. Even if he only gave you a cup of water in my name, he would be in the right. Sometimes I wonder about you two* (based on Mk 9:39–41).

Another time, the disciples spoke harshly to some people who were trying to bring children in to see Jesus (Mt 19:13–15). Church business is not the place for kids they insisted. Jesus was incensed.

Stop it! he said. *Let the children come here right now. Don't you realize that the Kingdom of God belongs to them?* (Mt 19:14) *Don't you realize that if you do not embrace the Kingdom like a little child, there is no way you will enter? What were you thinking?* (based on Mt 18:3)

Then Jesus took the children in his arms and blessed them.

I believe Jesus corrected people because changing your mind is critical to repentance. The Apostle Paul wrote, "Do not be conformed to this world, but be transformed by *the renewing of your minds,* so that you may discern what is the will of God—what is good and acceptable and perfect" (Rom 12:2, NRSV [italics mine]).

And, Jesus himself said, "[The Holy Spirit will] prove the world wrong about sin and righteousness and judgment" (Jn 16:8, NRSV).

Corrections are painful, but sometimes necessary to repentance. The Greek word for repentance itself, *meta-noia* (μετάνοια), literally means *mind-change.*

A change of mind is just as important as a change of heart.

Unplug Your Mind: If a relationship can't survive a correction, then how strong is that relationship?

Sometimes You Have to Rebuke Someone

A rebuke is harsher than a correction. It carries the connotation of condemnation. It is personal, and in-your-face. A rebuke is stronger than a scolding, a reproach, or even a reprimand. It is closer to castigate. It is also the language of exorcism. Jesus rebuked demons, fevers, and unclean spirits. He rebuked violent wind and raging sea. In other words, he challenged, defied, and broke the powers that cripple and destroy life. Through his rebukes he confronted and opposed that which afflicts and attacks humanity.

What is both fascinating and disturbing is that in addition to rebuking bad spirits (and bad weather), Jesus also rebuked three of his disciples. Ironically—as well as tellingly and disturbingly—the three he rebuked were Peter, James, and John. They were his closest friends and advisers, his inner circle. His most beloved received his most critical attention, his most harsh rebukes.

As strange as it may sound, during his final trek to Jerusalem Jesus sent messengers ahead of him to a Samaritan village (Lk 9:51–55). The envoy was to negotiate his staying there, overnight accommodations and such. But the village decided they did not want Jesus coming through there because "he was headed toward Jerusalem." That means either they were against helping pilgrims on the way to Jerusalem (wrong temple), or they were afraid that Jesus was going to Jerusalem to cause trouble and they did not want to be linked as accessories. No matter the reason, Jesus was not welcome there.

The Sons of Thunder, James and John, were furious about Jesus's rejection.

"Lord, do you want us to command fire to come down from heaven and consume them?" (Lk 9:54 NRSV).

Either they hoped to pray down lightning from the sky, or they had something along the lines of arson in mind. They weren't called the Sons of Thunder for nothing!

Jesus turned and rebuked them. The exact words of the rebuke are not revealed in the Gospel (Lk 9:51–55), but if it was anything like the ones Jesus hurled against demons and waves, he would have said, *Be silent!* What more, we cannot know. But of this we can be certain: Jesus was not interested in retribution against the town that turned him away. He saw

James and John's attitude and violent proposal in opposition to his message. Unintentionally, the Sons of Thunder had sided with the tempter, the evil one. Sure, they were defending Jesus, standing up for him, indignant at his mistreatment by the Samaritan village. They meant to be taking up for their leader and his cause. With the best of intentions, their loyalty and staunch support of him are admirable. But burning a village to the ground because Jesus was not welcome to spend the night there is just wrong. And for that, Jesus rebuked James and John as if they were Satan himself.

It seems a little unfair and heavy-handed of Jesus to correct them so strongly, but he was appalled by their proposal, and because he knew these two—and he knew they were not joking in the least—he lowered the boom.

Shut your mouths and put those matches away right now! Have you lost your minds? You are not acting like you are on the side of God. When did the evil one steal you from me?

Talk about disturbing the peace: Jesus did not spare them the full weight of his condemnation. *Rebuked.* It doesn't get much tougher than that. For James and John there is little doubt that this was difficult to handle—a low point for them for sure. How they dealt with it, or how quickly they snapped back, we cannot know.

It happened to Peter, too. Mark says Peter took Jesus aside and rebuked him but does not record what Jesus said (Mk 8:31–33). Matthew 16:13–23 also says Peter took Jesus aside and rebuked him, saying, "God forbid it, Lord! This must never happen to you," (NRSV) probably meaning, *Over my dead body!*

The context? Jesus had announced his decision to go to Jerusalem, where he would be rejected, tortured, and killed. This, of course, set Peter off, compelling him to pull Jesus aside and give him an earful. *That is the stupidest, most idiotic, moronic, suicidal thing I have ever heard!* In short, he thought Jesus's plan just plain stunk. And he told him so, privately it

seems, so as not to embarrass him too much in front of the
others. Poor Peter did not see the train coming.

In Matthew: He turned on Peter, saying, *Out of my way
Satan! You are an offense to me and to God, an obstacle to everything
I am doing. You know why, big boy? Because you've got your mind
all made up it's going to be a certain way, and God's way is incom-
prehensible to your thick skull* (based on Mt 16:23).

In Mark: The scene, and the message, is the same (8:33).

But Luke hit the delete key on the rebuking of Peter
by Jesus—meaning he omitted that part of the scene from
his Gospel—presumably because it is unseemly to have Jesus
treating his disciples with such disdain (Lk 9:18–22). The image of Jesus and Peter grabbing at one another and yelling at
one another is not for every audience. And though everyone
has the right when they encounter Mark 8 and Matthew 16
to change the channel, believe me, it hurt Peter more than it
hurts you.

For Peter, and for us as well, nothing could be worse than
remembering that Jesus said to the tempter in the wilderness,
"Away with you, Satan!" (Mt 4:10), for Peter was told by Jesus
at Caesarea Philippi to, "Get behind me, Satan!" (Mt 16:23)
There is no appreciable difference between these.

What could be more troubling than to know that the evil
one can use your best friend's tongue!

The more this sinks in, the more one sympathizes with
Luke's choice to omit the whole confrontation. The scene is
so alarming that perhaps Matthew and Mark should have at
the very least placed a warning label on it. Where is the pas-
sive, pensive Jesus that everyone assumes they know? Was he
having a bad day? Did that Jesus ever exist?

And what of Peter? In that moment did he actually become possessed by evil? Of course not. Like James and John
before him, Peter's intentions were good. Jesus had proposed
rejection, injustice, cruelty, and death. Peter could not just

lean back and say, *Oh yes, I see, that makes perfect sense.* He could not and did not. He stood up for justice, for righteousness, for life, and therefore for Jesus himself. All of Jesus's death talk seemed completely misguided to him, and Peter would have been dishonest had he not taken Jesus to task. Nonetheless, it was a dreadful scene. The raised voices. The accusations and ultimatums. It was undisguised and unrestrained conflict. No, Peter was not "possessed"; he was just human. God's way as outlined by Jesus stopped making sense to him. As the Apostle Paul wrote, *The cross of Christ is moronic to the educated, and offensive to the religious* (based on 1 Cor 1:23). The cross was basically the crux of all Paul believed, and he said it was the only thing he preached, but he knew that by human reckoning and reason it was just a crock. That is what Peter must have thought at Caesarea Philippi. This is a crock.

Maybe Luke's instincts were right. That scene is just too much. Conflict disturbs the peace, disrupts equilibrium, and threatens stability. What official church board would vote for anything that disturbed the peace, disrupted equilibrium, or threatened stability? Likewise, if Luke wrote his Gospel for a community of believers caught up in divisive conflict, what purpose would this combative scene serve?

On the other hand, Matthew and Mark kept it. So what was their reason? What was their message? Jesus did not shrink from the right even when it was certain to create controversy and misunderstanding. That is a message that all believing communities would do well to hear. More than that, the church needs to know its own origins: *The Gospel we preach, the message of the cross itself, disturbs the peace.*

It is not just Jesus's behavior that must be considered, but the good news of the Gospel itself: Jesus's teachings, the proclamation of God's kingdom, and the message of the cross itself all disturbed the peace—and continues to do so to this day. More than a mere disturbance, it is the crisis (*krisis* in Greek, meaning *judgment*) of the world: "And this is the judgment (krisis), that the light has come into the world, and people loved darkness rather than the light … " (Jn 3:19, NRSV).

The light came into the world, and we yet preferred darkness. The Son was sent in love, and the world hated him. Or as the Apostle Paul wrote, it is the wisdom of God that we in our ignorance deem offensive and moronic (1 Cor 1:23–24). This is no mere disturbance; it is a cataclysm. But that is coming.

There is yet another example of Jesus's disturbing behavior. Yes, he was known to correct people. Yes, he was known to rebuke anyone and anything that opposed his Father's will. But there came certain times, especially near the end of his earthly ministry, when Jesus went beyond correcting and rebuking. We turn now to the times when he mobilized an all-out assault. Feel for those he corrected. Pity those he rebuked. God have mercy on those Jesus targeted with his merciless onslaught.

Unplug Your Mind: Can your relationships survive a rebuke? Why or why not?

✓Sometimes You Have to Blast Someone

Damned, cursed, and shamed are words you will hear from Jesus in this section. These are his "woes." How to translate "woe" presents a problem.

When Jesus says "woe" to someone, scholars agree that it is an onomatopoeia, that is, a word that sounds like what it means. The word "woof," for example, is an onomatopoeia. It is the word for a dog's bark. It also *sounds* like a dog's bark. Same with the word "woe." "Woe" is the sound you make as an exclamation of grief. Saying it twice, as Jesus does in Matthew 11, increases the intensity of the expression. It goes beyond grief, beyond anguish, to an expression of utter shame, as the New English Bible translates it. Or as Lenski and others point out, "woe" is a grief-filled pronouncement of judgment and doom.[1] Thus, to paraphrase "woe to you" into something that captures the pain and desolation is important. The words that do that best are the ones you are about to read.

Now listen to the woes of Jesus, his anguish and condemnation:

Oh, you are damned, Chorazin! And you, Bethsaida, are damned as well! Even your ancient enemies the Canaanites would have repented if they had seen the works of power you have seen, and I wasted them on you. And you Capernaum, do you fancy yourself exalted because I lived here? No, you will find yourself in Hades. If Sodom had seen what you have seen, it would still be around today. Sodom is better off than you in the end! (based on Mt 11:21–24).

When Jesus pronounced his woe on Chorazin (a Galilean city above Capernaum), it was *descriptive* rather than *prescriptive*. That is, he described the condition they were already in. Jesus took their pulse, and he pronounced them dead on arrival. Jesus was *describing* their damned state—a condition they chose because they did not listen to him. He was not *prescribing* damnation—cursing them on the spot. [**FYI:** John's Gospel clarifies how judgment works. In John 3, Jesus conveys that, "those who do not believe are condemned already … " (Jn 3:18, NRSV). Self-condemned. He also said, "Do not think that I will accuse you before my Father" (Jn 5:45, NRSV). That bears repeating: *I will not accuse you before my Father.* He also said, "I judge no one" (Jn 8:15, NRSV). The point is that we judge ourselves depending on how we respond to the light of truth. And this judgment is not merely a future reckoning, but is a daily affair. Jesus said, "If anyone hears my words and does not keep them faithfully, it is not I who shall judge such a person, since I have come not to judge the world, but to save the world: anyone who rejects me and refuses my words has his judge already: the word itself that I have spoken will be his judge on the last day" (Jn 12:47–48, NJB). Jesus meant that either you believe him and his word or you don't. Did you trust the good news that Jesus fixed things up between you and God, and did you say "thank you" and enjoy the liberation? Or do you prefer the cold remoteness of a scorekeeping God? Would you rather rely on your own religious climbing to fix things up with him? That is the krisis/judgment of the world and how God's judgment works.

Chorazin, Bethsaida, and Capernaum were likely the towns in which Jesus was most popular and well received. If he cursed *them*, who is safe from damnation? Now hear this: *Cursed are you who are rich, for money is the only consolation you will ever get. Cursed are you who are well fed, for in short order you will starve. Cursed are you who are laughing now, because tomorrow you will know only sadness. Cursed are you when everybody says only nice things about you; your parents and grandparents had nothing but nice things to say about the phony prophets* (based on Lk 6:24–26).

Luke records these curses as a part of Jesus's Sermon on the Plain. In between blessings and teachings on love, Jesus pronounced damnation on the rich, the well fed, the giddy, and the popular. If *they* were all damned, who can be saved?

Where is the Jesus we learned about growing up? Jesus the timid and mild. Jesus the quiet and contemplative. Jesus the simple and self-effacing. Where is he? The towns that loved him most receive his coldest diagnosis. And between his words of blessing and love are the most severe pronouncements of damnation. How is it that the Jesus of Scripture is nearly unrecognizable to us—and especially those of us who grew up in church communities? How much of who Jesus was and what he really did has been censored to make it more palatable? How many well meaning but ignorant teachers and preachers suppressed large sections of the Gospels so that many of us who thought we knew Jesus come to find that we didn't know him at all?

Not so fast. The pilot has not turned off the *Fasten Seatbelt* sign. The curses of Chorazin, Bethsaida, and Capernaum were only warmups for Jerusalem. In Matthew 23 and Luke 11, Jesus spoke the upcoming words of condemnation to the faces of the temple authorities while in the hearing of the people of Jerusalem. He showed them up and made them look bad and on their turf. And he was going to get away with it at least for the moment.

There is a little noticed verse or two in John's Gospel that speaks to this: "Now some of the people of Jerusalem were saying, 'Is not this the man whom they are trying to kill? And here he is, speaking openly, but they say nothing to him! Can it be that the authorities really know that this is the Messiah?'" (Jn 7:25–26, NRSV).

Be advised. We have arrived at Matthew 23. Jesus has arrived in Jerusalem, and he's ready to lay it all on the line. The city will accept or reject him. There will be no in between. The rulers will have to embrace him or kill him. Knowing this, Jesus entered the city armed to the teeth. His tongue was as sharp as a two-edged sword (Rv 1:16), and—admit it—*sometimes you have to blast someone.*

You can do as the scribes and the Pharisees teach you to do, Jesus said, *because they teach from the authority of Moses. But don't do what they do, because they don't practice what they teach. They heap regulations on everybody, but don't expect them to lift a finger to help. Everything they do is for show; they carry bigger Bibles than you and wear longer robes. They love to sit at the head tables, to sit in the front row at the sanctuary, and to be addressed with respect around town* (based on Mt 23:1–7).

Jesus was warming up to more severe, descriptive pronouncements. The roller coaster has reached the top of the hill. There is only one way to go now:

You are already in hell, you scribes and Pharisees, you play actors and pretenders! When people try to live in the Kingdom of God, you always find a way to stop them, and you certainly won't live there yourselves.

Damnation is yours, hypocrites! You'll cross land and sea to make a single convert, but you convert him into twice as much of a child of hell as you are yourselves.

Curse you, you blind guides. You make people swear by the gold of the sanctuary, but it is the sanctuary itself that is sacred; you make people swear by gifts on the altar, but it is the altar that makes the gifts sacred.

Shame is already upon you, you fakes and phonies. It's unbelievable how meticulous you are to tithe every single penny that comes your way, but you don't give a damn about justice and mercy and faith. You could have practiced these without neglecting your precious tithe. But you are blind. You strain out a gnat while you swallow a camel!

Oh woe unto you, you imposters! The outside of your cup and plate are sparkling clean, but the insides are full of greed and self-indulgence. Blind fools! If you clean the inside of the cup, the outside automatically becomes clean.

You are completely damned, you charlatans and frauds! You are like whitewashed tombs, lovely and gleaming on the outside, but on the inside full of filth and death. You appear to be righteous, but it's a sham; inside you are full of duplicity and rebellion. You are like unmarked graves, and people walk over them. You are defiling people and they don't realize it!

Cursed are you, you cons and deceivers! You build and decorate tombs for the prophets, and you say, "If we'd been alive in their time, we would have never participated in persecuting them or shedding their blood." Baloney! It was your own ancestors who did that very thing, and you are just like them.

You are snakes! You are a tangle of pit vipers! Prophets, sages, and holy men are sent to you, and you chase them, persecute them, and even kill them! But later you'll boast of the lovely tombs you've built to honor them! Hell is where this train is going, and I don't think I can stop her (based on Mt 23:13–33 and Lk 11:44).

Who the heck would follow Jesus now? Those words made some important and powerful men want to kill him.

They also shed new light on what it means to want to be like Jesus, to follow Jesus, or to ask the incessantly popular question, "What would Jesus do?" Ask yourself this: Would *you* verbally attack those in religious and political authority? Would *you* wage war on them? Would *you* willingly await execution? Would *you*, though innocent, refuse to defend yourself at trial? Would *you* endure mocking, beating, and scourging? Would *you* allow yourself to be unjustly convicted, tortured, and executed as a traitor to your country?

Think about *these* things the next time someone asks you "What would Jesus do?"

Unplug Your Mind: What price are you willing to pay to follow the one who paid the ultimate price?

Conclusion

He corrected, castigated, and detonated at will, no matter where or when or who was involved. He exposed them with double-barreled blasts of truth.

Before moving on, we should not forget John's Gospel. Incidents of Jesus blasting the temple authorities are not exclusive to the Synoptics. [**FYI:** Matthew, Mark, and Luke are called "Synoptic Gospels" because of their many similarities in content and order. *Syn-optic* in Greek means *common view* or *viewed together*).] Far from it! Consider these blasts of truth from John's Gospel:

"I know that you do not have the love of God in you" (5:42).

"You know neither me nor my Father" (8:19).

"Why do I speak to you at all?" (8:25)

"You are indeed doing what your father does. You are from your father the devil, and you choose to do your father's desires. When [the devil] lies, he speaks according to his own nature, for he is a liar and the father of lies. Whoever is from God hears the words of God. The reason you do not hear them is that you are not from God" (selected verses from 8:39–47, NRSV).

"It is my Father who glorifies me, he of whom you say, "He is our God," though you do not know him. But I know him; if I would say that I do not know him, I would be a liar like you" (Jn 8:54–55, NRSV).

In short, John's Gospel should by no means be excluded from a discussion of Jesus's dangerous and brave assault upon the temple authorities in Jerusalem!

The next three chapters again take on Jesus's disruptive message. What he taught was no less effective or disturbing than what we have seen already. But his teachings—the words he spoke when not under scrutiny, pressure, or attack—give a brighter, clearer picture of what he meant by living in the kingdom, about having life abundant and eternal, and about the kind of self-ishness required to do it.

7

HE USED PARABLES LIKE A SIEVE

*"For this people's heart has grown dull, and their ears
are hard of hearing, and they have shut their eyes; so
that they might not look with their eyes, and listen
with their ears, and understand with their heart and
turn—and I would heal them."*

—Matthew 13:15

The following chapters will focus on the vital, central teachings of Jesus that are more often than not avoided or sanitized by writers and preachers. Having been so often skipped over and cleaned up, the sayings encountered here could well be unfamiliar. That being the case, Jesus's message may momentarily seem alien. Jesus himself may even be unrecognizable. However, what Jesus said and how he said it, even when it *is* familiar to a reader, can be disturbing. No one is safe! Keeping that in mind, a brief warning is in order.

Do not be surprised if something in these chapters is upsetting, because it covers things Jesus said that were upsetting by design. Simultaneously, you might be thrilled at the discovery of a "new" Jesus—the bona fide Jesus of Scripture. The latter would be a hopeful sign that this book is doing what it was intended to do.

Let us begin with a parable.

And You Call Yourself a Christian?

Perhaps the least familiar and most misunderstood parable Jesus told is the parable of the ten bridesmaids who took their lamps to go welcome the bridegroom.

But only half took oil with them, so when the groom was late and the night dark, the five foolish bridesmaids begged the others to share their oil. The reply? Go buy your own. We came prepared.

"We are in trouble here. We're out of oil for our lamps. How are we supposed to help you get the groom to the house? We could lose our jobs. Hurry, the groom is coming; give us some of your oil. We don't need much. Remember, we have to put food on our tables, too. Think of our families! Just a little oil. We'll pay you back, we promise. We can't afford to lose our jobs. Think of our children! Do you want that guilt on your conscience, knowing you could have helped, you could have shared, but you didn't? If you don't share your oil with us, shame on you! How can you be so selfish?"

"This is not our problem. We didn't mess up, you did. Besides, if we give you some of our oil, we might run out before we can get the groom back to the house, and then we would be in trouble. Go to the store and buy your own oil. You're not getting any of ours."

After they left, the bridegroom came, and those who came pre-pared took him to the house, where they bolted the door and began to party. Later the foolish five came knocking on the door and begging to get in. But the groom looked through the peephole and said, "Who are you? What do you want?" They said, *"It's us! Let us in!"* But he said, *"You're crazy. I don't know any of you,"* and he returned to the party.

Stay on your toes, because you don't know the time of his arrival (based on Mt 25:1–13).

Does something here strike you as strange in this parable? Nobody gets bailed out. Everyone is held accountable for her own preparation or lack thereof. Moochers are refused. And saying No to them was the right thing to do. They were ir-responsible. They blew it. They get no sympathy. No handouts. No entitlements. They suffer the consequences of their own failure. And why should anyone feel sorry for them? They made their beds. Do you recognize Jesus and his kingdom of heaven in this anti-moocher parable?

In his wonderful fable called "The Bridge," therapist and author Rabbi Edwin Friedman addressed the same theme.[1] My retelling of it here is a paraphrase of the original for the sake of brevity:

A man was crossing a bridge to a new life and a new start when he saw another man walking toward him uncoiling a rope from around his body. One end of the rope was tied around his waist. He handed the other end to the man going on to a new life, and then he jumped.

Hanging on for dear life, the man above yelled, "Are you crazy? I was going on to a new life, minding my own business, and you hand me this rope and jump. Why?"

The fellow dangling below yelled back, "Hang on. You're responsible for me now."

Yelling and blaming went back and forth for a while. The man on the bridge wasn't strong enough to pull the fool up. There was no place to tie off the rope, and he was getting tired. But if he let go, the stranger would die. It would be his fault!

He prayed desperately for an answer, and then ... Oh, divine inspiration!

He called to the man below, "Hey buddy, I'm giving you this one chance. Obviously I can't pull you up no matter how hard I try, but you sure as hell can climb! I'm going to count to 100. If you haven't climbed up by the time I get to 100, I'm letting go.

"1, ... 2, ... "

"Wait," the man below cried. "If you let go, I'll fall, I'll die, and it will be your fault!"

"19, ... 20, ... 21, ... "

"You're supposed to have compassion for others. You're supposed to care. You could save life, yet you'd let me fall to my death? How can you be so selfish?"

"61, ... 62, ... "

And the man below began to wail, curse, and gnash his teeth. He screamed every nasty word in the English language, and a few in various other languages. He spit and gestured obscenely and wailed and writhed at the end of his tether. But he did not climb. He could have, but he didn't.

"98, … 99, … 100."

The man on the bridge released his grip, let go of the rope, turned toward his new life and walked on, without guilt or remorse.

It is not fair to rewrite this zinger-of-a-fable in such an edited-down form. But what it provides is a parallel between the fable and Jesus's parable of the ten bridesmaids. The issues are essentially the same:

- A person or group who could and should take care of himself/themselves tries to get someone else to be responsible for him/them. (Give us some of your oil. Hold this rope.)

- The response is, that is your problem. (Go buy your own oil. Climb up.)

- The result is that the irresponsible ones suffer the consequences of their actions. (They are shut out of the wedding banquet. He falls to his death.)

A student in one of my pastoral care classes responded emotionally to the The Bridge fable and The Ten Bridesmaids parable. He told the class about a sister and brother-in-law who had been kicked out of the homes of several family members. He had taken them in out of pity. As a part-time pastor, he felt it was the Christian thing to do. He housed them and put them to work in his small, successful business. Within a matter of weeks he realized he was in trouble, and in a matter of months he had lost a valuable employee and his business was failing. What could he do? The student said something like, "I let go of the rope! I fired my sister and her husband, and kicked them out of my house." Crying at this point, he continued, "It was the most difficult thing I had ever done. And I really struggled with that decision. I've been unable to convince myself that I did the right thing. Now I know I did. If they wouldn't climb, I couldn't keep holding them up. The only alternative would have been to let them pull me and my family and our business down with them. I see that now. I did the right thing. But it was still the hardest thing I'd ever done."

What is Jesus teaching us about a true Christian approach—a kingdom of heaven approach—to those who won't take responsibility for themselves? Two statements:

One, I see clearly that you messed up and are in trouble. And two, No, I will not bail you out.

This works for managers, parents, senators, or any leader. This is the behavior of a mature Christian leader. It is always difficult, often painful, but usually best. Like parenting. If God does us the favor of letting us mess up, then why can't we do the same for our children? While sometimes painful, letting go of the rope is the loving thing to do for them. Failing and getting into trouble are unavoidable, so why make yourself sick and crazy over it? Let them feel the full weight of their failure or mistake; stop bailing them out (figuratively or literally, as the case may be!), and get on with life.

But what about the responsibility of Christian evangelism? How do people get the good news of God's salvation in Jesus Christ, and what is a Christian's role in telling the world about him? (Mt 28:19). In the parable, ten bridesmaids go out as partners and coworkers to do the work of the groom together. Bringing extra oil was everyone's responsibility, and babysitting those who failed to do so was not a part of the arrangement. The five wise bridesmaids say, *No, you cannot have any of our oil no matter what dire consequence may result from your own negligence.* The wise ones guided the groom to the house and entered with him into the party. But the others were locked out, and no amount of blaming or begging would change that fact.

Need we be reminded that it is God who saves, not us? *Christians* can save no one. We don't have the power, nor has God ever asked us to save anyone. The only person's salvation for whom we have responsibility is our own. It is between the believer and the Lord.

Yes, we Christians care about others. We make friends, witness with our lives; some of us even preach and teach and write and speak on the radio or TV; and always we pray that God will work for good in us and in those with whom we come into contact. We can tell the good news of Jesus and share his wisdom, encourage people to read the Scriptures for themselves, and live and proclaim salvation boldly. But that is the extent of it: We may offer the story, but the rest is up to God. We must have faith that God will use our meager, broken efforts to open ears and eyes, to change hearts, and to repair lives. To do more than this is to show a lack of faith in God to save, or even worse, to play God by manipulating and coercing belief. Does the name Jim Jones ring a bell? True and faithful evangelism never closes the door to choice. Without choice, evangelism becomes spiritual terrorism. What an oxymoron!

There is nothing Christians can do to *make* someone experience God's salvation. If someone doesn't want to know or believe, we have to be willing to accept it when they choose hell. Remember, most of us have been down there once or twice, and some Christian somewhere had the good sense not to bail us out. Otherwise, we might never have learned that hell is a pretty rotten place!

My Palestinian friends in Israel have a saying: "Mish mush kilty!" (Spelled phonetically.) I'm told that it translates to, "That's not my problem!" Christians would do well to learn this gem of a phrase and practice using it without guilt. The wise bridesmaids of Jesus's brilliant and difficult kingdom parable, though not in so many words, said that very thing. Kingdom living often requires one to say to whomever, wherever, "Laa! Mish mush kilty." "No! Fix your own problem."

Unplug Your Mind: When is it right to let people suffer the consequences of their irresponsibility? How does it feel?

Parables of the Kingdom of Heaven

Never ones for leaving stones unturned, Jesus's disciples once complained of his use of parables to teach: *Lord, why do you teach in parables?*, they asked.

The disciples voiced their concerns about Jesus's parables (Mt 13:10). Was he really keeping his audience and their limitations in mind? Peter and the rest were worried that if he talked over their heads, the people would feel stupid; and if they felt stupid, not only would they not understand, but they would not listen—could not listen. Was Jesus failing to get his message across?

If the disciples had twenty-first-century minds, they probably would have hired a big political consultant, a James Carville-type, to show Jesus an apostolic pie chart. It would have represented a survey of a sample population of Galileans, about half of whom, as the pie chart would show in red, did *not* understand his parables about the kingdom of heaven at all. They might have strategized a better approach for Jesus, a Plan B, one that would not insult the liberal elite in Boston while at the same time appeal to old Bubba down in Texarkana. They might have had Carville explain to Jesus that if he hoped to hone his message in time for the Passover in Jerusalem, he had better change his speech strategy now. Keep it simple stupid: *No more parables!*

But Jesus did not change his game plan. He insisted that the kingdom is a mystery, not a political platform or a campaign strategy: "This was to fulfill what had been spoken through the prophet: 'I will open my mouth to speak in parables; I will proclaim what has been hidden from the foundation of the world'" (Mt 13:35, NRSV).

Interestingly, the disciples often asked Jesus to explain parables to them privately because, we presume, they knew that Jesus would not explain them publicly. "With many such parables he spoke the word to [the people], as they were able to hear it; he did not speak to them except in parables, but he explained everything in private to his disciples" (Mk 4:33–34, NRSV).

He absolutely refused to explain it to anybody else.

> "To *you* (the disciples) it has been given to know the secrets of the kingdom of heaven, but to *them* (the crowds) it has not been given. For to those who have, more will be given, and they will have an abundance; but from those who have nothing, even what they have will be taken away" (Mt 13:11–12, NRSV [italics mine]).

When Jesus told parables, those who got it were ready to get it, and it would get clearer and clearer to them until their wisdom was overflowing. But those who did not get it would only become more and more confused. *That* is why he spoke in parables! It was so that they would look but *not* see. They will listen but *not* hear. He made sure that some would *not* understand. The parables were a filter.

> "The reason I speak to them in parables is that 'seeing they do not perceive, and hearing they do not listen, nor do they understand.' With them indeed is fulfilled the prophecy that says: 'You will

indeed listen, but never understand, and you will indeed look, but never perceive. For this people's heart has grown dull, and their ears are hard of hearing, and they have shut their eyes; so that they might not look with their eyes, and listen with their ears, and understand with their heart and turn—and I would heal them'" (Mt 13:13–15, NRSV; Is 6:9).

Why do Christians assume that Jesus's goal was to make everyone understand? The parables are proof that it was not.

The nature of the Kingdom is that it is coming and yet it is here. Once Jesus was asked by the Pharisees when the kingdom of God was coming, and he answered, "The kingdom of God is not coming with things that can be observed; nor will they say, 'Look, here it is!' or 'There it is!' For, in fact, the kingdom of God is among you" (Lk 17:20–21, NRSV). It is a mysterious reality. It is a secret. Who wants everyone to get it? Certainly not Jesus! That's why he told parables, nothing but parables. Like these:

The kingdom of heaven is like an insane farmer who throws seed in every direction. They land on the road, on the rocks, and in the briars. Not much makes it to fertile soil, but, oh, when it does, how glorious the harvest! (based on Mt 13:1–9).

The kingdom of heaven is like a mustard seed that someone sows in a field. It is the tiniest of all seeds, but it becomes one of the greatest shrubs, the size of a tree, so big that eagles can build their nests in it! (based on Mt 13:31–32).

The kingdom of heaven is like a woman who takes a pinch of yeast and mixes it in with three measures of flour, and the whole thing begins to rise! (based on Mt 13:33).

The kingdom of heaven is like a treasure buried in a field. Someone finds it, reburies it, then goes and buys that field! (based on Mt 13:44).

The kingdom of heaven is like a merchant in search of fine pearls.
When he finds the pearl of all pearls, he goes and sells everything he
owns to buy it! (based on Mt 13:35–36).

The kingdom of heaven is like a net thrown into the sea, that
catches every imaginable kind of fish so that the fishermen have to sit
down on the bank and sort the good from the bad. (based on Mt
13:47–48).

What is the meaning of these parables? There are four
significant truths.

First, it was not Jesus's goal that everybody get them. He
used his parables like a sieve to sift out those who did not
comprehend. In those who did not, their incomprehension
grew. And in those who did, their comprehension expanded.

Second, the disciples and religious leaders had a hard
time understanding that the kingdom of heaven is *here.* "For,
in fact, the kingdom of God is among you." [**FYI:** There
is a footnote in most translations of these verses that give
"within" or "inside" as alternative translations for "among."
The Greek is *entos* (ἐντός); (Lk 17:20–21)] In addition to the
kingdom coming on the last day, Jesus insists that it is here
among you, around you, and in you, and yet not everyone sees it.

Jesus often pointed to the hypocrisy of the Pharisees.
Most of them were not celebrating Jesus's ministry of teaching and healing. Yet if they had realized who he was or understood his announcement about the kingdom of heaven, they
would have been dancing and feasting, rather than complaining about all the dancing and feasting. (Mt 9:14–15) Luke put
it so well: "As [Jesus] came near and saw [Jerusalem], he wept
over it, saying, 'If you, even you, had only recognized on this
day the things that make for peace! But now they are hidden
from your eyes. Indeed, the days will come upon you, when
your enemies will set up ramparts around you and surround
you, and hem you in on every side. They will crush you to
the ground, you and your children within you, and they will
not leave within you one stone upon another; because you

did not recognize the time of your visitation from God'" (Lk 19:41–48, NRSV).

Jesus held Jerusalem as a whole responsible for failing to recognize the hour of his coming. Yet he saddled the religious leadership with the greater responsibility for that failure—especially the Pharisees, who should have known better. The word *blind* is in bold here for emphasis:

"I came into this world for judgment so that those who do not see may see, and those who do see may become **blind**." Some of the Pharisees near him heard this and said to him, "Surely we are not **blind**, are we?" Jesus said to them, "If you were **blind**, you would not have sin. But now that you say, 'We see,' your sin remains" (Jn 9:39–41, NRSV).

Jesus knew exactly what was going on in Jerusalem. Though the kingdom of heaven was in their midst, the blind were leading the blind, and the city was slip-sliding its way into Gehenna. [**FYI:** Gehenna in Hebrew is *Ge-Hinnom*, meaning the Hinnom Valley; this valley was the burning garbage dump and sewer, south and downwind of Jerusalem. It is one of Jesus's favorite metaphors for damnation and is often translated as "hell."]

I got a greeting card once with a quote from an unknown author. It read, "Those who hear not the music think the dancers mad." And that's what Jesus was to the Pharisees: a sinner (Jn 9:24), a glutton and drunkard (Mt 11:9), a demon (Jn 8:48), and a lunatic (Mk 3:21).

Third, Jesus was under pressure to do things the way his family wanted them done, the way his disciples wanted them done, the way the crowds wanted them done. Again and again he took stands that either disappointed or enraged. The use of parables is just one example. Concerned that his followers were not going to get it, the disciples could not understand why he used them (Mt 13:10). When they asked him to please just come right out and tell them what the kingdom is, Jesus stood his ground. It's called *self-differentiation*,[2] the ability to maintain a strong sense of self, to take stands that are unpopular when necessary, and to remain calm when everyone else is worried.

Fourth, Jesus never once said that the kingdom of heaven is a place where you go when you die. Of course that's what most Christians today believe. But it's not what Jesus said. According to him, we do not go to the kingdom of heaven; *it is coming to us!* In "The Lord's Prayer" he said, "Thy kingdom *come* (Mt 6:10; Lk 11:2). Moreover, Jesus only spoke directly about what happens when you die a grand total of twice (notwithstanding his debate with the Saducees about marriage in the resurrection [Mt 22:23–33], and his parable about a poor man named Lazarus [Luke 16:19–31]). The first instance, in John's Gospel, has Jesus as saying, "In my Father's house are many rooms; if it were not so, I would have told you. I am going there to prepare a place for you" (Jn 14:2, NIV).

Jesus promised his disciples that he was returning to his Father and that they would in their deaths and in the resurrection on the last day join him in "his Father's house." In the second instance, Jesus turned to one of the crucified men hanging next to him and said, "Truly I tell you, today you will be with me in Paradise" (Lk 23:43, NRSV).

In neither of these two cases did Jesus call what happens after death "heaven"; he used the words "my Father's house" and "paradise." In neither case did Jesus threaten anyone with punishment. In neither case was he descriptive. Neither did he connect "his Father's house" and "paradise" with his very brief mentions of "the resurrection of the dead," though he could have. The Bible, in fact, advocates not the traveling of your bodiless soul to heaven, but the resurrection of your body to immortality when heaven comes!

"So will it be with the resurrection of the dead. The body that is sown is perishable, it is raised imperishable; it is sown in dishonor, it is raised in glory; it is sown in weakness, it is raised in power; it is sown a natural body, it is raised a spiritual body. If there is a natural body, there is also a spiritual body" (1 Cor 15:42–44, NIV).

It was the Greeks and Romans who believed that when your body died, your immortal soul left your body and journeyed to Hades. This thoroughly pagan idea is contradictory to scriptural bodily resurrection. Almost inexplicably, Christians today prefer the pagan myth to scriptural truth when it comes to death.

Other than these two instances—when he spoke of "his Father's house" and "paradise"—he didn't cover the topic of life after death. That being the case, there is a problem. It is critical that we hear and digest this fourth truth about the kingdom of heaven: *that Jesus rarely spoke of what happens in death*.

Is it not true that many, if not most, sermons today are about what happens when you die? And is it not true that the result of this is that most Christians (and non-Christians) believe that Christianity is about securing your spot in the afterlife? This doesn't make sense. Jesus did not preach about what happens when you die at all! He preached about how to recognize, enter, and *live* abundantly in the kingdom of heaven.

The kingdom, as Jesus explained it in parables, is the mysterious eternal presence of God at work in the world: past and present and future; a reality recognized and entered by faith, one that transcends time and space and yet intersects time and space. He did not give instructions on what *death* would be like, but on how to enter the kingdom and *live*! He came so we could have life, and have it abundantly (Jn 10:10b). He spoke constantly of this. Seventy-seven times in sixty-eight verses in Matthew's Gospel alone the word "heaven" occurs. Yet not one of those instances has anything to do with what happens when you die! On the contrary, the majority of them have everything to do with how you live, here and now.

So why does sermon after sermon threaten us with the bad things that will happen to us when we die if we do not say "the magic Jesus words"? There is something *very* wrong when Christian leaders, who are supposed to be proclaiming what Jesus proclaimed—faith and life—are instead making their standard message fear and death.

I do not recall Jesus ever attempting to frighten people into turning to God. But I frequently read and hear about Christians who do that. I do not recall Jesus ever saying, "Come unto me, or you will die and God will punish you!" But I frequently hear or read these sentiments in Christian circles. It is so illogical and nonscriptural that it's difficult to fathom.

It seems that many Christians have resorted to using terroristic threats to "win souls" (and consequently increase church attendance and giving). They say things like, *God will punish you if you don't believe. This may be your last chance.*

When was it decided that a message of fear would be more effective than Jesus's message of faith in God's amazing grace? Are we really comfortable with using scare tactics as our primary method of evangelism? Do we have so little faith in the Holy Spirit to convict and convert? Why do pastors feel they have to shock people, or browbeat people, or sing the hymn *Just As I Am* for twenty minutes or more while they pressure people? This is insane. Such methods are actually a vote of "no confidence" in good news! They are undoubtedly a vote for bad news.

If God is love (1 Jn 4:8,16) and perfect love casts out all fear, then how can fear bring people to God? "There is no fear in love, but perfect love casts out fear; for fear has to do with punishment, and whoever fears has not reached perfection in love" (1 Jn 4:18, NRSV). Think about it. *Why did you become a Christian?* If you were trapped by fear-tactics, then you were not lured by love. Now, be really honest. Is the biblical gospel about love or fear? If it is about love, then does it not follow that much of Christian evangelism today is just plain messed up? Messed up how? It is *fear*-based and *death*-obsessed. It is invasive. It is impersonal. It is manipulative. It is extorting. It is dishonest. It is unbiblical. It is un-Christian.

There is another way, a less brutal and more biblical way. That way is the way of Jesus, who spoke of life and celebration, banquets and parties; he condemned religious hypocrisy and self-righteousness and unfolded the mysteries of faith in stories and images. Is that not good enough anymore? Is the "real" message too confusing or too frightening or too mysterious to be practical in terms of the all-important priority of church growth (whatever that is)?

It is definitely worth pondering. Is it not the cross that we are afraid of—that if we were to actually say what Jesus said, and do what Jesus did, that "the church" would be rejected, *be crucified* if you will, by the culture from whom it covets respect and acceptance?

Or maybe it's just that Christian leaders like their power—the power to hold the club of eternal damnation over the head of a smirking, disrespectful world. How cynical is that?

Unplug Your Mind: Is there anything you wish you could say to your pastor right now about his preaching?

Conclusion

Here is a summary of the four scriptural truths about the kingdom of heaven.

1. Jesus sorts out those who understand the kingdom of heaven from those who do not by speaking of the mystery in parables that he refuses to explain.

2. In spite of pressure to change his methods, Jesus risked confusing those around him by talking about the kingdom of heaven in parables only.

3. Those who understand the kingdom of heaven know that it is here among us, around us, and in us; those who see it are dancing, and those who do not are complaining about all the dancing.

4. According to Jesus, we do not go to the kingdom of heaven. It came, it is coming, and it is here with us. It is not about death, but rather life that is full and rich and real and abundant and overflowing eternally now.

Jesus used parables to strain out those who did not "get it," but he did not do that to judge anyone or pick on anyone or condemn anyone. He did not come into the world to judge it, but to save it (Jn 12:47b). Save it from what? From the yoke of a legal self-salvation scheme. How so?

Jesus said that your accuser is Moses (Jn 5:45) because the laws of Moses have become a curse. They were given in love to babysit (Gal 3:24) a people newly liberated from slavery in Egypt (The Book of Exodus). They were meant to secure their safety until God's law of love could be written on their hearts. The laws of Moses were never meant to be a means of earning merit before God. For if your commandment-keeping performance is what God chooses to judge you by, then you are lost. No one can keep the commandments. And if no one can keep them, then no one can be saved. All who try fail. That is why the law, good in and of itself, has become a curse.

For all who rely on works of the law are under a curse; for it is written, "Cursed be everyone who does not abide by all things written in the Book of the Law, and do them" (Gal 3:10 ESV).

Therefore, since no one can obey all the things in the law, no one can be saved by the law, and Moses the lawgiver becomes our accuser. Jesus said he would not accuse us to God (Jn 5:45). Our accuser is Moses who gave the law that cannot be kept.

Jesus's parables sifted those who received the kingdom of heaven's grace from those who refused it and were hell bent on earning their way by scorekeeping with the law. Either you want the Lamb of God who takes away the sins of the world, or you want the legal scales so that you can count your beans!

8

HE PROHIBITED BLAMING

*"To what, then, can I compare the
people of this generation?"*

—Luke 7:31

No matter how many times I read that thirty-first verse of Luke 7 I still hold my breath: "To what, then, can I compare this generation?" Jesus asked. He was preparing to summarize what his culture had become. It would be more comfortable to assume that Jesus was referring here only to the people of the first century. Then we could sit back and let him summarize *their* culture, not ours. Like it or not, however, by "this generation" I think he means to include us.

With his question he is preparing us for his view of what we are like. And that is an intimidating prospect at the very least. What is scary is that in Luke 7:31–34 he does it in a couple of sentences, and he describes us to a tee. And then later in Luke 13:1–5 he challenges our culture to the core.

You Are a Blaming Generation

Jesus gets very playful and parabolic in Luke 7:31–35. Yet playful and parabolic does not mean he will not pack a punch. On the contrary. He asks the crowd, *To what can I compare this generation? What are they like?* (based on Lk 7:31) Hold onto your hat. Here is Jesus's answer to his own question:

This generation is like children sitting on curbs and sulking around the neighborhood, whining to one another, "We played the flute for you, but you didn't dance; we cried, but you didn't feel sorry for us" (based on Lk 7:32).

What he said is that we are a blaming generation.

To further paraphrase Jesus's words: *This generation desires to control or blame. If the Son of Man can't be controlled, this generation complains, calls him names, and worse.*

Jesus announced that he did not come to jump when the world said jump or to hop at the world's bidding. Keeping the people happy and entertained meant nothing to him. The Son of Man does not operate by popular opinion polls. He does not pander. Even if he had tried to make them (us) happy, they (we) would not be satisfied.

Jesus pointed out that John the Baptist fasted and abstained from alcohol, eating alone and surviving on a strict diet of locusts and honey; people were certain he had a demon. But Jesus, on the other hand, ate and drank as he pleased and with whomever he pleased; everybody was certain he was a drunk and a glutton who condoned the lifestyles of sinners! (Lk 7:33–34) *How can you satisfy people like that?* Jesus is asking. If John is wrong for refusing to eat with anybody, then how can Jesus also be wrong for eating with everybody? You can't win with this generation.

This generation consists of children, Jesus concluded. They are not the children of God's wisdom, or they would not be such whiney blamers (Lk 7:35). They are children of another father. And he knows exactly whose children they are. Jesus said, "Why is my language not clear to you? Because you are unable to hear what I say. You belong to your father, the devil, and you want to carry out your father's desire. He was a murderer from the beginning, not holding to the truth, for there is no truth in him. When he lies, he speaks his native language, for he is a liar and the father of lies" (Jn 8:43–44, NIV).

We are a culture that can't understand Jesus and what he is saying because we have bought the lies. The evidence is all around us—in our families, our churches, and our culture. They are full of whiners and blamers, just as he described in Luke 7:31–34 above. And whiners and blamers are essentially liars. They lie to themselves about who is really responsible, and they lie about others to skirt the blame. The father of all lies would approve.

Here's an example: A counselor stopped working with whole families. Neither did he often work with the person identified by some in the family as the problem. He found that the only way to initiate lasting change in a family was to work with the strongest, not the weakest, person. It is the opposite of what you would think. In short, he wanted to coach the leader, the most mature person in the family. How did he determine the most mature person in one meeting with a family? "Easy," he said. "I look for the person who is blaming the least."[1]

The counselor looked for someone who was accepting his or her share of responsibility for the situation, who was doing the least amount of scapegoating, who was willing to work on doing a better job so that things would get better, and who was willing to face the truth about the family, no matter what that truth may be. Remaining a blaming victim yourself is the only way to ensure that you and your family will never heal or grow.

So blaming is the mark of weakness and immaturity. To work with the blamers is futile. Blamers cannot change. Why should they? They have it made. Nothing is ever their fault! But if you strengthen the leader in the "system" (the one blaming the least), then the whole system by osmosis begins to function better and the identified problem person can eventually demonstrate fewer symptoms. That is "systems therapy" in a nutshell.

If you had an argument with your spouse or someone very close to you recently, how much finger pointing did you do? How many of your sentences began with the word

"You?" As long as you are bent on assigning blame to the other, you will remain stuck in a cycle of immaturity and conflict. The issues will change, but the dynamic will stay the same. It is a hamster wheel of denial. It is a perverse cycle of blame. To stay there is to stay exactly where the evil one wants you. He wants you driven by blind fear, on a perverse quest for self-absolution that you will never ever get. The irony is that the only way to get real absolution is to see the ways in which you are responsible for your life so that you can receive forgiveness and go live.

The Bible is full of blaming characters. We have already seen one of them. For thirty-eight years the paralyzed man sat beside the Pool of Bethesda, and when Jesus asked him whether he wanted to be well, the man whined, *Somebody always gets into the pool before I can. Can't you see that I'm a crippled victim?* (based on Jn 5:6–7). Thirty-eight years on the hamster wheel with no serious thought of getting off. Every day for thirty-eight years: stuck in the same place, same result, same excuses, never his fault. *I don't have anybody to help me.*

Chapter 1 began with two brothers at odds over an inheritance. *It's my brother's fault for not sharing the inheritance with me, Jesus. Help me prove it by ruling in my favor* (based on Lk 12:13). Show me someone who sues frequently, and I'll show you someone on the hamster wheel of blame.

The five foolish bridesmaids failed to bring oil. They might have blamed the five wise ones for not reminding them, or for not bringing extra just in case. They might have blamed the bridegroom for coming before they could weasel their way out of the situation. Likewise, in the bridge fable, the man dangling from the rope could have climbed up rather than blame someone else for his predicament. But he was so sure it was not his fault that he would have rather died than stop blaming! Can it be that blaming is so powerful and pervasive in our culture that there are people who would rather die than stop?

Back to the Bible: Elijah walked all the way to Mount Horeb (Sinai) and sulked in a cave. The Lord asked him what he was doing there, and he said, *Look at all I did, killing the 450 prophets of Baal, and still the Israelites break your covenant, smash your altars, kill your prophets, and now, after all I've done for them and for you, they are looking to kill me too. I think I'll just sit in this cave and die!* Even great prophets have their whiney, blaming moments! (based on 1 Kgs 19:9–10).

Job's wife had a handle on the blame game. Job was afflicted with a terrible skin disease, but he did not blame anyone. He nursed his wounds as best he could without one word against anyone including God. After a while, his wife could not keep quiet anymore: *Job, I can't believe you're still holding on to your integrity. Just curse God and die like everybody else. Get it over with* (based on Jb 2:7–9).

Here is my favorite example of blaming in the Bible: God asked Adam, *Did you eat from the tree I told you about?* And the first words out of his mouth are "The woman." He said, *The woman whom you gave me picked it and I ate.* And it is not only the woman's fault for picking the fruit, but it is *God's* fault for making the woman in the first place! (A line from Jimmy Buffet's song, Margaritaville, comes to mind: "Some people claim that there's a woman to blame ... ") And of course Eve is no better. She blames the serpent. (And by they way, who made the serpent?) (Gn 3:11–13) From the beginning to now, it has always been someone else's fault.

Jesus's indictment of us—*yes, us*—as a generation of blamers is right on target, which makes his simple little analogy about children all the more disturbing. He said that this generation is "like children sitting in the marketplace and calling to one another, 'We played the flute for you, and you did not dance; we wailed, and you did not weep'" (Lk 7:32, NRSV). He could not have been more accurate. We do not lead; we complain. We do not accept responsibility; we point fingers.

We absolve ourselves through gossiping and scapegoating and lots of vengeful suing. We are a generation of spoiled children.

Just look at the nauseating parade of afternoon talk shows and courtroom shows featuring whining, pathetic, blaming, chair-throwing "victims" Jerry and Montel and Geraldo are rich and famous today only because our culture enjoys watching adults act like children. And there are so many blamers willing to do that on national television that the talk show hosts should all be set for life.

Growing up and becoming an adult means a transition away from blame toward responsibility—a move from immaturity to maturity, dependency to independence. But if Jesus is right, we are a generation of big babies—babies with mortgages and nuclear weapons. Try not to think about that for too long.

The argument still rages today over who is to blame for Jesus's death. That is how immature we are. Some misguided haters blame the Jewish race. Some blame just the Jewish authorities of Jesus's day. Some blame Rome. In fact, several individuals did their part. Caiaphas, the high priest, played his trump card, as we shall see. Judas, one of the twelve disciples handpicked by Jesus, betrayed his master's whereabouts for thirty pieces of silver. The rest of the disciples were too blind to see the betrayal coming, and when it did come they all ran for their lives, abandoning Jesus to his fate. There is plenty of blame to go around.

Yet, as I see it, the whole human race had its hand in the rejection of Jesus. The light came into the world but people preferred darkness (based on Jn 3:19). And at the same time, Jesus too had a say in his fate. He said, *No one takes my life. I give it. I have the power to lay it down, and the power to take it up again* (Jn 10:18). He accepted responsibility for his decision. And if Jesus blamed no one for his own tragic execution, how can we spend our lives blaming others for much more trivial matters?

Unplug Your Mind: Can you think of anyone in your family, church, or organization who does *not* make a habit of blaming?

A Preacher Who Won't Blame

The easiest thing in the world is to preach about hot topics, as most pastors would admit. There is nothing tough about scoring brownie points with a congregation by ranting about something that scares or upsets them. It's easy to bash abortion. It's simple to slam homosexuality. It's effortless to rave against violence in the media.

Pulpit pandering doesn't really require a lot of brains, energy, or courage. Actually, it is a cinch: It is low risk, and it scores high with many congregations. And this kind of paranoia preaching contributes to the blaming that consumes our generation. When the preacher stomps on some activity or group, it is possible to feel immune—even superior—and thus avoid the unpopular biblical stance that calls for personal responsibility.

Jesus had an amazing opportunity to play that game—as good an opportunity as any preacher could hope for. What he did with it, however, is shocking.

Jesus, there's been an atrocity, someone from the crowd reported. *You're from Galilee, right? Well, there were some Galileans worshiping, and Pilate's men butchered them during their prayers, and their blood flowed and mingled with the blood of their sacrifices!* (Lk 13:1)

It was a slow pitch across the middle of the plate for Mark McGwire. A grand slam waiting to happen. Jesus had an attentive crowd and despicable news just begging to be condemned. Why not knock it out of the park? These were his brother Galileans massacred at prayer! Go ahead Jesus: Slam Pilate's men, slam Pilate, slam the Emperor, and slam Rome. The crowd will go nuts. Take those murderous cowards apart!

Galileans did have a reputation for being rebels, and one perspective is that Pilate's soldiers gave them what they deserved. But of course asking Jesus to pass judgment on the event was a trap. They had set a snare for Jesus, similar to the one about paying taxes to Caesar (Mt 22:15–22). In that situation, it looked like Jesus would have to choose to be anti-tax or pro-tax. Either way he loses. Same here. It's a damned if you do, damned if you don't scenario. If Jesus condemns Pilate, he is another Galilean rebel. If he says the rebels got what they deserved, then he is a Roman collaborator.

The crowd looked to him, waiting. He gazed from eye to eye through the crowd. Presently he spoke, asking them a question:

Do you think that these Galileans deserved what they got? Do you really think they were worse sinners than all the other Galileans?

Silence.

Absolutely not, he said. *But unless you live a repentant life, a similar death is exactly what you can expect.*

Jesus raised his voice above the murmuring:

Or those eighteen workers on whom the tower at Siloam fell, did they deserve to die because they were being paid money stolen from the temple to build Pilate's aqueduct? Were they worse offenders in the eyes of God than everyone else in Jerusalem that day? Absolutely not! But you will all be likewise crushed if you are unrepentant (based on Lk 13:1–5).

Extraordinary. When given an opportunity to pander to an angry, attentive audience, Jesus showed his mettle. He did not condemn the action of Pilate's men. Nor did he credit

God with punishing the Galilean rebels. Instead he leveled his gaze right at the crowd, and warned *them* of the peril of an unrepentant life! Why did he do that?

Because an unrepentant soul finds it easy to speak of the evil of others—Galileans, Romans—and ignore the evil in his own heart. That is what will truly and finally condemn. That is self-damnation. The unrepentant do not take responsibility for their own souls.

Jesus showed no interest in fanning the flames of anger, of riling them up, of taking a populist stand. Jesus had the audacity to refuse to play the blame game over Pilate or the rebels, and instead he challenged his audience's *own* presumptions of innocence.

Are all of you not responsible for one soul and one soul only? Pay attention to yourselves! Receive salvation and forgiveness. Repent. Otherwise it might as well have been you that got sliced up by Pilate's men or crushed under a falling column of stone.

Imagine the outrage: *Me repent? I did not murder worshipers. Pilate did. I did not line my pockets with stolen temple money. Those workers did. How dare you tell me to repent! Did I kill those who knelt in prayer? Did I steal from God's treasury?*

And Jesus's likely reply: *No, but if you keep bellyaching and blaming, while neglecting repentance in your own heart, you might as well have. You can choose whichever road to hell you like.*

To a generation of sulking, spoiled, little brats who point and blame and pout and snivel, Jesus holds up a mirror. He will not contribute to their immaturity. Jesus was notorious for practicing what he preached. He drew the line, and it is altogether likely that those who heard him that day were resentful. But he did not seem to care. Not at all.

Our Lord could have hit that slow pitch deep into the left field bleachers. He could have circled the bases pumping his fist. Standing ovation. Deafening cheers. Emerging from the dugout to tip his cap to adoring fans. Instead, he reached out, caught the ball, stuffed it in his pocket, and warned each and every one of them to go get a life before it was too late.

Unplug Your Mind: Blamers love a preacher who blames, but how are they going to feel about one who won't?

Conclusion

Though Jesus never used the word explicitly, it succinctly captures his assessment of this generation: *blamers*. Our immaturity still shows. The alternative, of course, is to take responsibility for our flaws and failures, looking honestly at ourselves and acknowledging that we are part of the problem. Refusing to blame means refusing to get on the hamster wheel of self-absolution, refusing to point fingers. In other words, Jesus banned blaming. That is a start. And he never said it would be easy.

Did you know that Jesus has the answer to how not to blame? He taught us and showed us. It's been in the Scriptures all along. Jesus taught us and showed us all about standing, following, and dividing. Blaming doesn't stand a chance.

9

HE CALLED BELIEVERS
TO STAND, FOLLOW, AND DIVIDE

"... one's foes will be members of one's own household."
—Matthew 10:36

Listen to Christian radio talk shows. Read editorials written by ministers in local papers. Sure, they are condemning the ills of society, taking a stand for what's right. But are they merely doing what Jesus refused to do? Are they slapping around easy targets for the sake of their own popularity?

A distinction needs to be made: There is taking a stand, and then there is grandstanding. Sometimes these can be confused. Jesus refused to grandstand. Pandering to audiences by whacking around an easy target was not his idea of preaching. But there were times, many in fact, when he took a stand. What about his condemnation of the scribes and Pharisees, their hypocrisy and self-righteousness? A stand or grandstanding? How do we tell the difference?

The best way to begin to discern what's preached from what's practiced is to look at a central tenet of Jesus's teaching and then look at how he actually *lived* it. As Jesus approached Jerusalem it was his intent to make a final stand. To distinguish this final stand from grandstanding, it helps to compare what he did with what he had been saying. So let us take a look at one of the most familiar and most misunderstood teachings of Jesus: cheek-turning. And we'll see if Jesus walked the talk.

An Alternative to Fight or Flight

Jesus taught that if struck on the cheek, one should offer the other (Mt 5:39). Turning the other cheek equals letting people walk all over you, right? Someone attacks you, and you do nothing. You repress the impulse to strike back. They win. Is that what this is about—being a doormat for Jesus? Spineless, gutless, wimps for Jesus? How inspiring! Maybe there is another way to understand what Jesus meant.

The instinct for fight or flight in the animal kingdom is an example of what Jesus did not teach. Animals, no matter how evolved—even chimps or dolphins—have no capacity to reflect on their response to danger. They flee or they stay and fight. (Some creatures play possum, but that is just a variation on fleeing. To hide, in essence, is fleeing that does not involve breaking a sweat.)

This fight-or-flight behavior is also evident, obviously, in the human species. We are often reduced to animals when under attack. Brain experts these days label the three major sections of the human brain as the reptilian brain, the mammalian brain, and the human brain.[1]

First, look at the reptilian brain.

In the back of our skulls is a part of the brain that—in function, chemical makeup, and design—is reptilian. It is a primitive structure compared with the human frontal lobe. The reptilian brain is the part that fires up when we are threatened. It does not reason. It tells one to slither or strike. That is all snakes know how to do.

Three interesting things about reptiles is that they don't play, they don't nurture, and they don't communicate vocally.

Reptiles have no capacity for batting around a ball of yarn. They have no capacity to tend lovingly to their offspring. They do not have complex vocal signals at their disposal. There are exceptions to these three, to be sure, but the descriptions work for metaphorical purposes.

So if you have a reptile in your organization (and who doesn't?), he will be humorless, heartless, and irrational. This is helpful for understanding the de-evolved among us, as well as our own capacity to de-evolve under stress. Super-seriousness, cold-heartedness, and unreasonableness are fundamental animal attributes of the human mind. The reptilian brain in all of us is capable of deadly serious, irrational cruelty. That is how snakes, lizards, and alligators have survived these millions of years. They are ruthless, relentless, and remorseless.

The more sophisticated mammalian brain is in the middle of our skulls. It is capable of play, nurturing, and vocal communication. But if a mammal sees a tiger—even if that mammal is as intelligent as a chimp—it still does not have the option to pause and reason which course of action might be best. It just climbs the nearest tree! Fight or flight are still the only two options for non-human mammals, even though they possess more evolved brains than reptiles.

What makes the human brain unique is the frontal lobe. Specifically, the neocortex. It has the power to regulate reactivity from the more primitive neural firings of its less evolved mammalian and reptilian components. It has the power, but *ability* requires conscious effort and years of practice.

Keeping your sense of humor when you are being harassed by a coworker does not come naturally. Remaining rational while your teenager is throwing a tantrum does not come naturally. Communicating calmly and clearly when everyone else is in panic mode does not come naturally. These are the skills of a highly evolved neural structure. And even the best at it are unable to regulate their animal reactivity more than 66 percent of the time.[2] One third of the time we are overwhelmed by the baser instincts of the more primitive mammal and reptile within us. We fight or flee.

Back to "turning the other cheek." You may have guessed that *that* is the third option. Turning the other cheek might be called simply standing. It is the highly evolved alternative to fighting and fleeing. And Jesus was the master.

Turning the other cheek is not running away. It is a refusal to be intimidated or to be run off. It is standing your ground and facing the animal that is attacking you.

Turning the other cheek is not getting even either. It is a refusal to use irrational, unnecessary force, and it is also a refusal to go away, to back down from what's right. Turning the other cheek is standing your ground in the face of raw, naked, reptilian aggression—and not giving an inch.

At Gethsemane, when the officials with torches and weapons came to arrest Jesus, Peter fought and then fled. Most of us would have done one or both given the circumstances, I suppose. But what of Jesus?

Jesus prayed in agony for hours before his arrest. The trial of deciding whether or not to stand is very real. He may have considered rallying the people for a military attack on the Romans. He had the crowd's support by all accounts, and many already assumed he had come to Jerusalem to take the throne of David. On the other hand, Jesus certainly must have considered fleeing. The walk from Gethsemane east, away from Jerusalem to the top of the Mount of Olives, takes about twenty minutes. Over the top and down into the Judean wilderness and its crevices and caves would mean complete safety in only an hour, two at the most.

Jesus could have fought or fled. Instead, he stayed. He stood. He did not back down. Yet he did not strike. He did not hide behind his disciples. He stood alone in the open when the mob came for him.

Jesus confronted the soldiers, temple police, scribes and Pharisees, and asked them, *Who are you looking for?* They answered, *Jesus of Nazareth.* Jesus said to their faces, *I am he* (based on Jn 18:5).

John's Gospel includes a wonderful detail at this point in the story. When Jesus said, *I am he,* John says they were so

stunned that they stepped back and tripped over themselves
and fell! Jesus, still standing his ground, asked them again. *Who
are you looking for?* Again they said, *Jesus of Nazareth.* And Jesus
replied, *I told you I am he. So if you are looking for me, here I am.
Let these others go* (based on Jn 18:4-8).

Luke also says that Jesus calmly addressed the mob: "Have
you come out with swords and clubs as if I were a bandit?
When I was with you day after day in the temple, you did
not lay hands on me. But this is your hour, and the power of
darkness!" (Lk 22:52–53, NRSV).

Then things headed south fast. They must have grabbed
Jesus because Peter started swinging his sword, and Jesus
screamed at him to stop, and then the disciples all panicked
and fled. The "brave men" arrested Jesus, bound him, and
took him away (Mt 26:36–58; Mk 14:32–50; Lk 22:39–54;
Jn 18:1–14).

But Jesus was not through showing how to turn the other
cheek. They hauled him before the high priest for prelimi-
nary questioning. When he was grilled about his teaching and
his disciples, Jesus replied: "I have spoken openly to the world.
I have always taught in synagogues and in the temple, where
all Jews come together. I have said nothing in secret. Why
do you ask me? Ask those who have heard me what I said to
them; they know what I said" (Jn 18:20–21, ESV).

He was standing again, ever standing. Turning the other
cheek. Not backing down. He would not resort to hate or
abuse, nor would he be run off. He was not going away. Ever.
He would have his say, and they would have to deal with the
strength of his righteous stand.

When Jesus had finished speaking, one of the temple policemen hit him in the face (Jn 18:22). He did not like the "disrespectful" way Jesus had addressed the high priest.

Jesus looked unflinchingly at the guard and said, "If what I
said is wrong, bear witness about the wrong; but if what I said
is right, why do you strike me?" (Jn 18:23, ESV).

Though this moment may have never been described in these terms before, it must have been a turning point in the "proceedings." There was no hiding it anymore. It was clear as never before: *Jesus was the strongest person in that room and, though bound, he was the only truly free person in that room.* He couldn't possibly be more dangerous. Whatever resolve they had to dispose of Jesus was most certainly hardened in observing that exchange. They must have felt as though a lion was roaming loose through Jerusalem, hunting and stalking them (Is 31:4).

It takes no extraordinary strength to fight or to flee. What takes strength is to stand. Could you have stood your ground in Gethsemane or before the high priest and his vicious policemen? Turning the other cheek is wimpy? Hardly. Nothing could be further from the truth. Jesus taught it and practiced it.

That is how we tell the difference between standing and grandstanding. Jesus chose to suffer when he did not have to. Recognition was irrelevant. Reputation was irrelevant. Doing the right thing was worth suffering for; he stood his ground, and he would not back down.

By the way, does anyone miss the unexciting, uninspiring, uninteresting, vanilla Jesus who continues to haunt our cultural imagination? I don't. OK, Jesus was humble, gentle, lowly, and reverential (Mt 11:29). But that did not make him a milquetoast invertebrate!

Time and again Jesus demonstrated that he was supremely self-confident, strong-willed, and sure. Possessing a brilliant mind and quick wit, wielding a razor-sharp tongue and nerves of steel, with white-hot zeal and unfailing faith, with the use of daring assaults and heroic stands, Jesus demonstrated why his Father loved him from the foundation of the world (Jn 17:24).

Unplug Your Mind: Can a real man love Jesus?

Some Things You Must Hate

Have you ever seen a pastor turn someone away, or at least warn them of the danger and difficulty of actually following Jesus? If not, something is way off.

Jesus discouraged people from following him, and we need to look at why he did that. What did he say, and what was he concerned about?

Crowds were traveling with Jesus as he headed for Jerusalem; the entourage was getting larger and larger. Jesus turned, looked back at all of them as they followed him down the road, and said: *Go home if you do not hate your father and mother. You cannot follow me.*

Stunned silence. He continued.

Go home if you do not hate your wife and kids, and your brothers and sisters. You cannot follow me.

Go home if you do not hate your own life. You cannot be my disciple.

Can any of you carry the cross? Go on home. You have no idea of the price you must pay.

Go home. Following me will cost you everything. Your family, your home, your possessions. None of you can be my disciple if you cannot do this (based on Lk 14:25–33).

As if it is not shocking enough that Jesus would warn people not to follow him, then we have to deal with something far worse. Who is really a Christian? By the standards Jesus outlined here, who can say with confidence, *Yes, I hate my parents, my spouse and kids, brothers and sisters, house and possessions, my very life, and I can carry my cross?*

Some would soften this by saying that what Jesus means is you should love him so much that all other loves are like hate in comparison. But we should be suspicious of those who water down the Gospels. I admit that we have to respect that Matthew's Gospel softens the tone. He records Jesus saying, "Whoever loves father or mother more than me is not worthy of me" (Mt 10:37). The word hate is gone. It is replaced with the phrase "loves more than me." But we still must deal with Luke. Allow his words to sink in. There is no fuzziness, ambiguity, slack, or wiggle room: If you want to follow Jesus, you must *hate* everyone and everything, even your life. This is your cross. Carrying it means taking your truth-stand against reptilian attack even if it costs you dearly. If you cannot do this, you cannot be a disciple of the Lord.

Unplug Your Mind: If you had to write a church newsletter article on Jesus's warnings about following him, what would you say? Is there any chance it would get published?

The Prince of Peace?

Here is Jesus's most dreaded, most wonderful saying of all. There is no easy or comfortable way to approach this. Face-to-face, no place to hide. In Matthew 10, Jesus warns that all disciples who follow him will make enemies of their own families. "Brother will betray brother to death, and a father his child, and children will rise against parents and have them put to death; and you will be hated by all because of my name" (Mt 10:21–22, NRSV). Yes, following Jesus will expose enemies in the ranks in your home.

Based on Matthew 10:16-36, this paraphrase gives a crowd's eye view of Jesus warning his followers of the danger of loving him.

Now that you've signed on, I am going to send you out like sheep in a pack of wolves. Prepare yourself for attack. It will happen. I want you to be as innocent as doves, but you will be living among wolves. You'll need to be as shrewd as a snake.

They will arrest you and humiliate you. You could end up in jail, or before a judge or governor. If this happens, don't prepare a statement or a defense. The Father and I will help you when the time comes.

You won't know who to trust. Your brother, father, and children could all betray you. And you will be hated by everyone. No one will defend you, and no one will care.

What? Are you surprised? They are doing it to me, and they'll do it to you, too. They call me the prince of demons! What makes you think you will be immune if you chose to live in my house?

It's going to be bad, but don't be afraid. They think they are in the right by abusing you, but their hypocrisy will be exposed.

So here are your orders: What I'm telling you in the dark, you go tell it in the light! What you hear people whispering in secret, go shout it from the rooftops! Expose them, and everything false and evil they say or do.

What can they do? God will take care of you. Even the hairs on your head are valuable to him.

Don't chicken out on me either. If you do not acknowledge me to others, how can I acknowledge you to my Father.? Do you think that my instructions will disturb the peace? Listen carefully: I did not come to bring peace to the earth! I came with a sword. I came to divide. Wherever you go you will cause division because of me. There will be no peace, not even in your own homes.

I'm here to set a man against his father. I'm here to set a daughter against her mother. Daughter-in-law against mother-in-law.

Your real enemies aren't out in the countryside somewhere. Because of me, you will find your enemies in your own household! And they are far more dangerous to you than the wolves.

So, don't pull any punches, especially with your family. Expose it all. Tell it in the light. Shout it from the rooftops. Shake up the world. And do not be afraid. I am with you, and so is my Father.

If you know anything about Superman comics, TV shows, or movies, you may remember the term kryptonite. Kryptonite is what they call the green rocks from the planet Krypton, the home planet of Superman. On earth, the only thing that can harm him are those *poisonous rocks from home.* Think about that for a moment. Let it register. The only thing that can destroy Superman are *those poisonous chunks from home.*

Guess what the New Testament Greek word for *secret* is? It's *krypton*— κρυπτόν ! That is exactly the name of Superman's home. Coincidence? I doubt it. The creator of Superman probably had this very thing in mind. Jesus did, too. Jesus warned his followers about the poisonous secrets from home—deadly even to a man of steel—with the power to destroy body and soul.

Look at it again. In Matthew 10 he said: "Brother will betray brother to death, and a father his child, and children will rise against parents and have them put to death ... [there is] nothing secret that will not become known ... and what you hear whispered, proclaim from the rooftops ... fear the ones who can destroy both body and soul in hell ... and one's [enemies] will be members of one's own household" (Mt 10:16–39).

What do people pay counselors for if not to expose the family secrets that are killing them? What do families fear more than anything else, if not those poisonous secrets? Why do families fear and even attack those who want to talk about the dark past? From Scripture, why did Jesus's kin *really* reject him, try to stone him, believe him to be insane, and try to put him away quietly? (Lk 4:28–30) Why did the people of Gergesa *really* want Jesus to leave after the wild man from the tombs became clothed and in his right mind? (Mk 5:17) We could keep going with this, but the point should be clear: The poisonous secrets from home are far more dangerous than any pack of wolves.

Families will go to extraordinary lengths to keep the krypton hidden. That dark stuff, that dirty stuff, that great, deep and buried grief, that unclean history cannot be allowed into the light—or so families seem to believe. They see the krypton as a devouring monster that must be caged in the basement. Chained up like the demoniac in the tombs outside of town.

The irony is that by burying the secrets, they are poisoning their own yard. But it does not matter in the end. No one can hide it forever, according to Jesus: Nothing is covered up that will not be uncovered, and nothing secret (**κρυπτόν**—*krypton*) that will not become known (Lk 12:2, NRSV).

The truth will win out one way or another. And when it escapes, sometimes there are emergency room bills. Sometimes there are even mortuary fees.

So what did Jesus mean when he said that he came with a sword, not to bring peace but to divide? To set family members against one another.

The Scriptures are clear. Jesus did not come into the world to keep it as it was. He did not come to smooth things over, to please everyone, and to leave things the way he found them. To the contrary, he came to make a difference.

Jesus made a difference by making waves. He rattled the cage. He disturbed the peace. Yet as important as it is to note that he shook up the world, it is equally as important to note where he did the shaking: He chose families and synagogues. Kin and congregations. That is where he seemed to be convinced that the world must be purified by flame. He exclaimed, "I have come to set the earth on fire, and how I wish it were already blazing! (Lk 12:49, NAB).

Kin and congregations. He rocked both, and he rocked them hard. For anyone brave enough to read his words, he still rocks them. To Jesus, the worshiping of the sacred family was no different from any other kind of idolatry. *Put your family first*, it is said. Yet Jesus said:

Your enemies are in your own home. (based on Mi 7:2; Mt 10:36) and *Who are my mother and brothers?* (based on Mt 12:48; Mk 3:33) and *Put the kingdom of God first* (based on Mt 6:33).

Any Christian and any church that make a difference will cause a disturbance among kin and congregation. It is unavoidable. And it is God's command. We are not to repress secrets, but to expose them (Mt 10:27). We are not to stay home and play it safe, but to go out there and tell it like it is (Mt 28:18-20). We *will* pay a price for doing this, but our cross is something we are supposed to be carrying anyway (Lk 9:23).

Unplug Your Mind: If Jesus didn't come to bring peace to families and churches but to divide them, then how can conflict and division produce good in these organizations?

Conclusion

Lord, give us Jesus, unplugged. His seven most vital teachings have for too long been avoided or censored:

1. Christians are not obligated to bail out irresponsible, immature people.
2. Christianity is not about what happens when you die.
3. Christians should not tolerate blaming.
4. Christians should not tolerate pandering.
5. Christians must stand up to bullies.
6. Christians hate their lives, their kin, their belongings; and they carry their crosses.
7. Christians disturb the peace and welcome conflict.

Fantasize for a moment about what would happen if your minister or priest preached this message. Even though Jesus preached them, it is still hard. Try anyway, if you will. Visualize him or her standing in the pulpit of your local sanctuary. Hear each of the seven statements above proclaimed to your congregation. Let the words hang in the air for a moment. Let them echo around the room. Are you nervous? Maybe that's why the impact of Jesus's words is so often cushioned or altogether avoided.

As I see it, Jesus threw the world a really beautiful, nasty, dancing knuckleball. And the Christian world has been trying to turn him into a straight fastball pitcher ever since.

10

MESSIAH DAMNED

"Christ redeemed us from the curse of the law
by becoming a curse for us—for it is written,
'Cursed is everyone who hangs on a tree.'"

—Galatians 3:13

The title of this final chapter is "Messiah Damned" with very good reason. That reason begins with these two clues—a *Messiah* and a *tree*.

First, the tree: Deuteronomy 21:23b reads, "Cursed is everyone who is hanged on a tree" (ESV). Did you know that? The Apostle Paul did. He wrote about it to the churches of Galatia: "Christ redeemed us from the curse of the law by becoming a curse for us." Where? On a *tree*, meaning the cross on which he was crucified. Hold that thought.

Second, the Messiah: The chief priests and elders of the Jewish court (the Sanhedrin) found Jesus guilty of being a false Messiah. [**FYI:** *Messiah* is a Hebrew word meaning *anointed one*; Messiah becomes *Christos* (Χριστός) in Greek, then Christ in English.] Some slapped him saying, "Prophesy to us, you Messiah! Who is it that struck you?" (Mt 26:68, NRSV) But notice that they did not stone him for religious blasphemy as one might expect. Instead, they took him to the civil court of Judea, to a Roman named Pontius Pilate, for a civil trial.

Notice during that trial what the prefect of Judea asked the chief priests and elders. Pilate asked, "Then what should I do with Jesus who is called the Messiah?" All of them said, "Let him be crucified!" (Mt 27:22, NRSV).

Then, as he was being crucified, the chief priests stayed near the cross of Jesus and shouted so that all could hear: "Let the Messiah, the King of Israel, come down from the cross now, so that we may see and believe" (Mk 15:32, NRSV).

The only clues you need are there: a Messiah and a tree. If you do not understand what the temple leaders were up to yet, that's OK. You will.

But there is a bigger plot at work here. The larger question is, What was *God* up to? That's what Chapter 10 is all about.

A City with Cancer

Why didn't they just stone Jesus to death? Jewish capital punishment was stoning, not crucifixion—not during that period anyway.[1] The Judean leaders could have handled the trial and execution themselves, though John 18:31 seems to contradict this: "Pilate said to them, 'Take him yourselves and judge him according to your law.' The Jews replied, 'We are not permitted to put anyone to death'" (NRSV).

Yet there are many examples from that period of Jews contemplating and exercising capital punishment by stoning. Not the least of these would be biblical examples including Peter's second trial (Acts 5:33), Paul's remarks before Agrippa (Acts 26:10), and the account of Stephen's stoning (Acts 7:57–60). Rome actually gave the temple officials authority to slay any foreigner who trespassed the inner courts of the Jerusalem temple. They posted inscriptions at every gate in Greek that read,

> *"No outsider shall enter the protective enclosure around the sanctuary. And whoever is caught will only have himself to blame for the ensuing death."*

Fragments of these inscriptions have been found and are part of the archaeological record.

Stoning is mentioned many times in the New Testament. Jesus saved an adulterous woman from stoning (Jn 8:7). The leaders and the crowds tried to stone Jesus himself several times (Lk 4:29; Jn 8:59, 10:31, 11:8). Paul claimed to have been stoned once (obviously he survived or was resuscitated) (Acts 14:19; 2 Cor 11:25). And Jesus once called Jerusalem, "the city that kills the prophets and stones those who are sent to it!" (Mt 23:37). Clearly the Jewish authorities could stone lawbreakers.

Nevertheless, John wrote that "the Jews" (the Judean authorities in the Jerusalem temple) were not permitted by Rome to "put a man to death" (Jn 18:31). That is simply not true. And Pilate would have known that. Perhaps what he meant was that they, the Judeans, were not allowed to try and put a man to death *for a capital, civil crime*. Prefects of Judea, including Pontius Pilate, almost certainly would have reserved the right to handle capital, civil crimes, that is, cases dealing with sedition and rioting. That being the case, the Judean leaders' plan becomes even clearer.

Had the religious authorities stoned Jesus—as they did Stephen later—it would have been for blasphemy, or crimes against the temple, or profaning Yahweh or the Sabbath, or other possible charges, real or trumped up. And had they done so we might have rocks rather than crosses in our sanctuaries! But the Judeans were clever. They knew exactly what they were doing.

The assembly of the elders decided on two goals. First, not to merely get rid of Jesus, but to completely discredit him. Second, to arrange it so that the crowds would not blame them. How could they kill two birds with one stone? That is where the Romans came in.

The elders knew the law. Deuteronomy 21:23 clearly states that anyone hung on a tree is under the curse of God. " ... for anyone hung on a tree is under God's curse" (Dt 21:23b, NRSV).

To put it more vulgarly, anyone who dies on a tree or whose corpse is hung on a tree, according to Deuteronomy 21:23, is *God-damned*.

So, how did the elders plan to discredit Jesus's messianic claims? Apparently they reasoned that if they could get Jesus crucified—*killed on a tree*—then God would damn him. And since God cannot damn his own Messiah, it would prove that Jesus of Nazareth was not the real Messiah. This was their plan to expose him as a pretender. And if, as he was being crucified, they were to gather around to mock him as a fraud, to make sure that the crowd received a strong dose of Scripture disproving Jesus's claims, then not only would he be dead, but everything he did, taught, and claimed would also be obliterated. That was the plan. Stoning would merely kill him. Crucifixion would erase him.

But how would they get him crucified? What Roman law had he broken? What if they were to change the charges from blasphemy to sedition? Jesus spoke of "his kingdom." His followers hailed him as the son of David, their "king." And since there is no king but Caesar, they reasoned, was not this troublemaker guilty of sedition? They planned to witness to Pilate that Jesus was a subversive, an insurrectionist, a troublemaker, and a rabble-rouser who stirred up the people and called himself king. If they could get *that* charge to stick, he would be sentenced to death by Rome, meaning crucifixion, and it would be all over for him.

Stoning Jesus themselves would have been quicker and easier. But the officials had a concern: The crowds were with Jesus. If the Judeans themselves were to execute him, there would be much risk to their families, their offices, their nation, and themselves. If the people were to riot, Rome could come down on their heads, and Jewish rulers could lose the generous autonomy Rome afforded them in their own affairs. Moreover, they could lose their lives. But, their plan to change the charge to treason against the Emperor, were they to get a conviction, would end the Nazarene's life, discredit his claims, and remove their blame for his conviction and execution. It would be the will of Rome!

Please allow me to mix two metaphors here. Jesus called the Judean leaders snakes, a brood of vipers. And reptiles have already provided a helpful metaphor for their coldblooded actions against Jesus. But cancer also works as a metaphor for the Judean council.

Cancer consists of singleminded, relentless cells. Some cancers do not recognize the boundaries of neighboring cells, and are invasive and sabotaging. Others just drain neighboring cells of lifegiving blood. Cancer is a once normal and healthy cell that has lost its purpose, its specialty, and its individuality. A cancer cell is completely self-serving. It is not "conscious" of the damage it is doing to the host body. Yet as it successfully proliferates, it slowly kills the host on whom it is dependent for survival. This behavior in human terms is evil, pure and simple, and whether we are talking about at the cellular level or at a human organizational level, evil works the same way. It will destroy an internal organ or an organization in exactly the same way.

Overall success rate in the fight against cancer is about the same as the success rate in organizations getting free from the grips of meddling, sabotaging, cancerous bullies: about 30 percent.[2] That doesn't sound very promising. But if you are in an organization with cancer, that is some measure of hope. There is a one-in-three chance "you might lick this thing." That is better than none.

> "Jerusalem, Jerusalem, the city that kills the prophets and stones those who are sent to it! How often have I desired to gather your children together as a hen gathers her brood under her wings, and you were not willing!" (Mt 23:37; Lk 13:34, NRSV).

Perhaps Jesus had a one-in-three chance of curing Jerusalem of cancer. The chemo he provided was potent and toxic. *Woe to you, woe to you, woe to you!* He fed the truth into the bloodstream of the city, and the city reeled from it. *You snakes! You brood of vipers! You blind fools!* But in the end, Jerusalem's immune system may have been too weakened, the cancer too widespread. Too advanced. Judging from his own predictions of what would happen, Jesus must have suspected the outcome (Mt 16:21; Mk 8:31; Lk 9:22). But he took his stand nonetheless. He did that because his stand was not merely for the purpose of curing Jerusalem of cancer. That would have been a nice result. But he had a larger purpose.

Unplug Your Mind: How do you stop a meddling, spreading, sabotaging, or stealing person, and how will he respond when you do it?

Clarity Made Him a Target

Jesus, as we have seen, had a remarkable sense of himself. By that I mean he was not swayed by opinion or pressure. He was not particularly concerned about being liked or acting in ways that insured his popularity. He acted and spoke out of an inner clarity of self, and functioned in tune with that clarity. To put it biologically, he was a healthy cell, highly specialized and differentiated. He had an identity and a purpose. He refused to dance when people played. He refused to overfunction. It did not bother him to disappoint, and he did not mind saying No.

However, it is not often appreciated that there is an intense loneliness that accompanies this kind of leadership quality. Jesus's checking out with or without his disciples is evidence of the toll that this kind of leadership takes. People surrounded him all day, yet simultaneously he was alone. He found his strength in his clarity of self and purpose, knowing who he was, what he would do, and what he would not do.

It is not often appreciated that such clarity is born of struggle. Jesus struggled mightily in the wilderness, tempted by many possible futures, all of them lobbying hard to win. He struggled when he retreated to the north, to Caesarea Philippi, to pray about his next step. He struggled even up to the last minute, in Gethsemane, where he looked for another way. Jesus's clarity did not come cheap. It was born of sweat like great drops of blood falling to the ground.

Through loneliness and struggle, Jesus realized where he was going. He had vision. He could see it and articulate it, and he made it clear to everyone what he was going to do. Jesus was intent to teach and heal, to go to Jerusalem to confront the temple authorities, and to be arrested and killed. And though his closest associates did not approve (Mt 16:22; Jn 11:8), they followed with amazement and fear (Mk 10:32). Jesus had a destination, and though they warned him not to go, it made no difference (Lk 13:31). With dark irony and yet deep purpose Jesus said, "it is impossible for a prophet to be killed outside of Jerusalem" (Lk 13:33).

Returning to our "brood of vipers" metaphor for a moment, it is a fact that reptiles are drawn to heat and motion. That is a metaphorical way of saying that those who know who they are and where they are going draw the attention of saboteurs. Strong leaders generate energy and action within an organization, and that lures the "cold-blooded." They see movement and heat, even in the dark. My point? Clarity of self and clarity of vision, while essential for strong leadership, are *precisely* what make a strong leader a mark.[3]

Healthy cells in your body go through a process of differentiation and specialization. In other words, a "good" cell comes to distinguish itself from other cells, and comes to have a purpose. A healthy cell knows what it is and what it is supposed to do. Cancer cells and other pathogens are just the opposite. They do not differentiate or specialize. And, perversely, they can be drawn to attack cells that do!

Please pardon again the mixture of metaphors here, but they work. For a long time the Judean authorities had been looking for an opportunity to get rid of Jesus. They showed their scales when they used an informant to find out where he was spending the night, going by cover of darkness to arrest him while the crowds were not there to protect him. They bided their time and hunted for an opening to take down the man they couldn't look in the eye in broad daylight.

So, arguably the number-one and number-two essential qualities for leadership are clarity of self and clarity of direction. And while few things are 100 percent true, this is: Strong leadership triggers sabotage.[4] It was true for Jesus right from the start. Jesus was tracked and attacked in the synagogues, in the streets, and at home. His heat and motion were irresistible to their reptilian sensors. Their eagerness increased in Jerusalem as they lay in wait, calculating their strike. Jesus agonized through the night in Gethsemane because he saw their nocturnal ambush coming.

God had given him clarity, but clarity had made him a target.

Unplug Your Mind: How do you get clarity of self and clarity of purpose, and why do you want it?

He Was Giving Self Away

Target or no, and in his determination to go to Jerusalem to confront the religious leadership, Jesus seemed to become less cautious. We hear no more of him going anywhere in secret, no more checking out for private time, no more orders not to tell anyone what he had done or who he was. He refused to listen to his disciples, who complained that he should not even go to Bethany because of its proximity to Jerusalem (Jn 11:8). He mocked Pharisees who were on his side when they warned him to leave before Herod caught him (Lk 13:32–33). He rode in on a donkey in broad daylight, refused to quiet the crowd, wrecked the temple, and set his disciples as guards at the entrances (Mt 21; Mk 11; Lk 19). He railed against the leadership, cursing their hypocrisy (Mt 22-23). Jesus was emboldened by his clarity, and by his impending death.

Not that Jesus's actions in Jerusalem were inconsistent with his earlier Galilean ministry. He stood strong against the forces of evil while in Galilee, too, subduing the wind and the waves, casting out demons and illness, and confronting the hypocrisy of leaders in the synagogues and their human traditions. He had been standing up to evil all along. The difference in Jerusalem was that he was making a final, decisive stand against the people at the top. No more stealth or caution. No more privacy or secrecy. But this was not for show.

Rock musicians through the years have worn crosses, using messianic lyrics and stage props for their concerts. Jesus and the cross make dramatic images on stage. Performers use them to capture attention, which is of course part of what they are paid to do. Rock is in part about showing off, attention getting, even shocking the audience. The musicians sometimes even use Jesus or his cross to promote themselves, the very opposite of what Jesus was doing. Or was it?

One might argue that Jesus was an attention-getter, an egotist, and a showman, no different from the performers today who go to extremes (intentionally or unintentionally) and gain notoriety. It might have even appeared that way to those who witnessed his last days in Jerusalem. Perhaps Jesus of Nazareth was just a narcissistic rabbi. Maybe he was another traveling evangelist addicted to the spotlight. Perhaps he was another false messiah consumed with self-promotion and self-aggrandizement. Maybe he was pulling a publicity stunt to rally the people for a military coup.

But conclusions do not fit the evidence. By every account, for Jesus, it was about giving himself away. He willingly gave up hope of having safety or respectability. He let go of ambition, popularity, and prestige. *Those who cling to life will lose it. And those who let go of life will find it* (based on Mt 10:39, 16:25;

Mk 8:35; Lk 9:24, 17:33; Jn 12:25). He willingly died in naked humiliation and failure.

The Apostle Paul put it like this: "Let the same mind be in you that was in Christ Jesus, who, though he was in the form of God, did not consider equality with God as something to be exploited (or grasped), but emptied himself, taking the form of a slave, being born in human likeness, and being found in human form, he humbled himself and became obedient to the point of death—even death on a cross" (Phil 2:5–8, NRSV).

This stand Jesus took, this turning the other cheek, this refusing to fight or flee, was not attention-seeking behavior. In fact, it was the opposite. The key here is that Jesus was seeking *nothing* for himself; he was denying himself. He was giving self away. And he had a reason.

At the end of the film *Braveheart*, William Wallace is in prison, awaiting his morning public execution where he would be strapped to a horizontal cross, splayed and gutted alive. He knelt in his cell and prayed: "I am so afraid. Give me the strength to die well."

Unplug Your Mind: What is your idea of "dying well"?

The Mystery of Jesus's Cross

On a Monday morning, about a hundred students listened to the German theologian, Jurgen Moltman, reading excerpts from his upcoming book in a thick accent. Many students brought extra large coffees. That morning, when the caffeine was just starting to wear off, Moltman said something like, "In the cross, we find God forsaking God." It was one of those moments a student of theology and Scripture will not soon forget.

The cross attests not only to the strength of Jesus, his clarity of self, and his clarity of purpose. It also testifies to the

strength of God. God refused to over-function at Gethsemane. God forsook his Son. Jesus was not abandoned, but he
was forsaken for a season. God allowed this to happen without stopping it. And, if the incarnation means anything at all,
let this sink in: *God actually did not interfere in the killing of God.*
That would prove Jurgen Moltman correct. In the cross, God
truly was God forsaken. In forsaking Jesus, God forsakes himself incarnate in the Son's flesh. If ever there was a time God
should have been tempted to over-function, it would have
been to stop the crucifixion of Jesus. But no. The Son was allowed to suffer and die, and in that God too suffered and died.
It sounds crazy. But there is no other logical conclusion, since
the Son and the Father are one. "For in [Jesus] all the fullness
of God was pleased to dwell" (Col 1:19, NRSV).

So in a real sense, if all the fullness of God was in the Son,
then the cross of Jesus is the Father's self-giving, too. All that
God is was given away in his Son. Forsaken. Sacrificed. In
that moment, it was not *we* who made sacrifice to God, but
God who actually sacrificed God's self to *us* through his Son.
This is a radical departure from the sacrificial systems of all
religious traditions, including ancient Palestinian Judaism, and
a complete reversal from the religious norm. Who ever heard
of a god sacrificing to people? It is wonderfully ridiculous.

But there's more. The crucifixion was God revealing his
humility. God absorbed the very worst that we, his own creation, could dish out. Almost everyone knows a little bit about
the cruelty of Roman scourging, the weight of carrying a
crossbeam tied to your shoulders, the shock of being nailed
to it, and the extended torture of hanging on it. In those final moments, God in Jesus relinquished all claims to power
and wealth and wisdom and might and honor and glory and
blessing (Phil 2:6–7; Rv 5:12–13). He emptied himself. The
Father, in unity with the Son and the Spirit, willingly became
poor on the cross. The emptying of Jesus was the emptying of

God. We killed God the Son, and he used that very moment to forgive us.

This cross was God's choice because of his loving, humble, sacrificial nature. It was his great pleasure to give the kingdom to humanity as a gift (Lk 12:32); and that was his Son's exact nature and purpose. The Father and the Son share that nature with the Spirit. And the Father, Son, and Spirit share that loving, humble, sacrificial unified embrace with the entire human race, born and unborn.

When the very Eternal Word of God in the flesh hung damned on a tree with arms wide open to *all*—he drew *all* people to him (Jn 12:32). Humanity became God's because sin and death and damnation were removed as obstacles to God in Christ's gracious embrace.

God in Christ saved us apart from laws and rules and deeds and sacrifices and prayers and religion (Rom 3:28). He saved us by sheer grace, pure and sweet, so that *all* are forgiven while they are sinners; that proves God's love to everybody (Rom 5:8). In the Son's flesh God has made all into one. He has abolished the law, with its commandments and rules, to create in himself one new humanity. He made peace, reconciling humanity to God in one body through the cross rather than our good behavior. And *all* are members of the household of God, built on the foundation of the apostles and prophets, with Christ Jesus himself as the cornerstone. In him the whole structure is joined together and grows into a holy temple. In him you also are built together spiritually into a house for God (Eph 2:14-22).

That is what the Bible calls "good news." Through Jesus God was pleased to reconcile to himself all things, whether on earth or in heaven, by making peace through the blood of his cross (Col 1:20, NRSV). The battle is over. We no longer have to fight our way back to God. He fought his way to us. His kingdom came and is coming and will come, and nothing can stop it.

Just as Jesus said No to foes, friends, and family, the cross was his final No to the world. It says, No, I will not accept your blindness; No, I will not accept your darkness; No, I will not allow sin and death to separate us; No, I will not allow your failed efforts to obey God's laws to condemn you. Therefore, in Christ and his cross there is no separation. In Christ and his cross, there is no condemnation. *All* are in Christ Jesus (Rom 8:1). In him we *all* live and move and have our being (Acts 17:28).

The result is strange and marvelous. It is a mystery. As Robert Capon said, "Now heaven is entirely populated with sinners saved by grace, ... and hell is entirely populated with sinners saved by grace."[5]

It is good news that Jesus saved the whole thing. It is good news that he forces no one to believe it, or live in it, or enjoy it. It is good news that some will enter gladly and join the celebration of life abundant. The tragedy is that some will choose to the bitter end to not enjoy this mega-party even though they are already in attendance. That is a hell of a shame.

How many parties, dinners, celebrations, and banquets are mentioned in Luke 14 and 15 alone? Nine! The whole point is to celebrate and come home. Why? For some reason God has a passion for finding that which was lost. A single sheep is found: Throw a party. A single coin of little value turns up: Throw a party. One disrespectful wayward son comes home: Throw a party. What can humanity do? What can the universe do? The Trinity wants to party!

We are free. We do not have to look busy and serious about seeking God. God is not the one who is lost. It is God who comes for you and risks all for you and gives everything to you and throws the best party ever for you. Many people seem to understand this and go on into the party and have a wonderful time. However, there is always at least one who enters the ballroom and stands in the middle of the floor refusing to dance, refusing to eat the cake, and refusing to drink the champagne (Lk 15:28). That must be pure hell.

Is there any sense in which we might speak of the crucifixion of Jesus as God's chemo for the world? The truth, the love, and the sacrifice of God's own life embodied in his Son, shot into the veins of his dying planet?

How are the healthy cells responding? How are the cancer cells responding?

Unplug Your Mind: What more could God have done to communicate his undying love for the world?

The Scandal of Jesus's Cross

The Apostle Paul claimed to preach a message that is both scandalous/offensive and moronic/foolish. What was that message?

"For the message of the cross is foolishness to those who are perishing, but to us who are being saved it is the power of God. For it is written,

'I will destroy the wisdom of the wise, and the discernment of the discerning I will thwart.'

"Where is the one who is wise? Where is the scribe? Where is the debater of this age? Has not God made foolish the wisdom of this world? For since, in the wisdom of God, the world did not know God through wisdom, God decided, through the foolishness of our proclamation, to save those who believe.

"For Jews demand signs and Greeks desire wisdom, but we proclaim *Christ crucified*, a **stumbling block** [*skandalon*— σκάνδαλον in the Greek—is the root of our English word scandalous; it also means offensive] to Jews and **foolishness** [*morian*— μωρίαν in the Greek—is the root of

our English word moronic] to Gentiles, but to those who are
called, both Jew and Greeks, Christ [is] the power of God and
the wisdom of God.

"For God's foolishness is wiser than human wisdom, and
God's weakness is stronger than human strength" (1 Cor 1:18–
25, NRSV).

Christ crucified. Does that strike you as strange? Christians
comfortably speak of Christ crucified all the time. What is offensive or moronic about saying Christ crucified?

Christ is the word that replaced the term Messiah in the
Greek-speaking world where Paul took the Gospel. So we
are talking about the Messiah (God's anointed) being crucified. Now take note of Deuteronomy 21:23 (and Gal 10:13).
It says that God curses/damns anyone hung on a tree—and
therefore anyone crucified. Are you putting it together now?

Christ crucified is a Greek way of saying Messiah damned!

Sounds offensive, does it not? Sounds moronic too. How
could an intelligent, prudent man like Paul preach Messiah
damned? How can God's anointed one be damned by God?
It does not make a lick of sense.

But Paul made no apology. He was not ashamed of the
Gospel (Rom 1:16). He believed it was true precisely because
it was too outrageous not to be. He, like so many after him,
believed it because no one but God could come up with
something so spectacularly ridiculous! [**FYI:** It is a long-time
mystery. For almost 2,000 years people have wondered what
circumstances would cause a person or persons in the Corin-
thian church to proclaim "Jesus be cursed."

("Therefore I tell you that no one who is speaking by the
Spirit of God says, 'Jesus be cursed … '" [1 Cor 12:3a, NIV])

Paul has no problem whatsoever with the phrase "Christ
crucified," though it means "messiah damned." But Paul *did*
have a problem with changing it to "Jesus *be* cursed." He
warns that no one speaking by the Spirit of God can say that,

because it is not *we* who curse him. He subjected *himself* to God's curse. Furthermore, changing it to *"Jesus* be cursed" eliminates the most important word—*messiah*—so that you totally miss the punch line: that the Gospel—that "messiah damned"—is both true and an oxymoron.

"Jesus be cursed" was probably a modification of "Christ crucified" ("messiah damned") used by some in worship in Corinth as an ecstatic exclamation. I do not think they meant any harm. They probably saw it as consistent with what Paul preached. If they were being intentionally inflammatory or divisive, I believe Paul would have hammered them. But his censure is mild. He does not even tell them to stop. All he says is that it is not of the Spirit, meaning it is not compatible with the Gospel he preaches, which is "Jesus Christ and him crucified" (1 Cor 2:2, NIV).]

So the Sanhedrin's plan to erase Jesus's claim to Messiahship by having him cursed on a tree turned out to be the wisdom of God? What the Sanhedrin meant for evil, God intended for good? (Gn 50:20).

Messiah damned. Offensive? Yes, in the extreme. Moronic? Yes, absolutely. But as Paul wrote, "For since, in the wisdom of God, the world did not know God through wisdom, God decided, through the foolishness of our proclamation (Messiah damned), to save those who believe" (1 Cor 1:21).

In the current climate of political correctness and hypersensitivity, it is as if we are surrounded by "the offended." Christians today are not immune to this "don't offend" trend. We have joined the ranks of the hypervigilant. Not to offend is casually seen as a Christian duty.

Yet how do we reconcile our political correctness with Jesus? Jesus offended people. His teachings and behaviors offended people. And the Bible comes right out and says so. His own kin and hometown folks took offense at him (Mt 13:57; Mk 6:3). The Pharisees took offense at him (Mt 15:12). His own disciples took offense at him (Jn 6:60-66).

Paul even said the Gospel is offensive! Specifically, he wrote that the Gospel message of "Christ crucified" was a stumbling block to Jews, meaning an *offense* to religious sensibilities (1 Cor 1:23). In other words, the message itself is experienced by many as offensive. Paul referred to Isaiah in Romans 9:33: "See, I am laying in Zion a stone that will make people stumble, a rock that will make them fall, and whoever believes in him will not be put to shame" (NRSV).

"A rock that will make them fall" can be translated "a rock of offense." The Greek word for "offense" is the same in all the preceding paragraphs: *Skandalon*, meaning stumbling block is the root of our English words scandalous and it means "offensive."

While the message is admittedly scandalous to some, particularly to the religiously hypervigilant, Jesus made it clear that one need not experience it as so. Jesus said, "blessed is anyone who takes no offense at me" (Mt 11:6). And Paul clearly wrote that to those being called by God, the message of Christ crucified (Messiah damned) is *not* moronic or offensive, but is the power of God and the wisdom of God (1 Cor 1:24). "For God's foolishness is wiser than human wisdom, and God's weakness is stronger than human strength" (1 Cor 1:25).

This is what Jesus is all about, according to Paul. And that is not preached and taught very much today. How so? When the subject of Jesus comes up, arguably the most common response is to start talking about "doing right" and "straightening up" and "trying harder" and "getting back to church" and "stopping drinking."

People feel shame and guilt at the mention of Jesus's name rather than forgiveness and freedom!

They should feel understood and liberated and empowered. They should feel wonder, awe, and delight. Instead, when Jesus is mentioned, they too often start talking about "getting right with The Man before I die." Hopefully, this book will change some minds. That is what "repent" literally means, "to change one's mind" (μετάνοια—*meta-noia*—change-mind).

Unplug Your Mind: How can you live in and communicate to others this moronic, offensive good news?

Conclusion

The decisive battle between good and evil took place almost 2,000 years ago in Jerusalem. Jesus brought his clarity of self and his clarity of purpose to bear on the religious and political leadership of Judea. That clarity made him a target of seething attacks. Jesus won every debate and won the popularity of the crowds, yet he drew intense hatred from the leaders he humiliated.

At the height of his popularity they plotted Jesus's demise. Why? Because he was wrong and his teachings were false? Not at all. It was because he was right, because he told the truth, because he exposed their hypocrisy, and because he threatened their popularity, prestige, and power. The provocative Jesus provoked them, as he must. He drew them out into the open. And there he slew them with his double-edged sword of truth.

With cancerous cruelty and reptilian cunning they arrested him. But binding him did not rob him of his freedom. They beat him, but it did not rob him of his strength. They mocked him, but it did not rob him of his dignity. They found him guilty, but it did not rob him of his innocence. They killed him, but they did not rob him of his life. The world's hate could not rob him of his forgiving love.

Everything they did to him backfired. Every attempt to weaken him made him stronger. Every attempt to erase him made him ever more indelible.

It is too strange and wonderful to be true. The Judean authorities' master plan to erase Jesus was to get him crucified and thus damned by God (Dt 21:23). And the message that his first believers embraced was exactly that—*Christ crucified, Messiah damned!* Who but God could have planned something so brilliantly absurd?

A God-damned Messiah saves the world. Offensive. Moronic. Provocative. *Perfect.*

So the authorities' decision not to stone him, but to get him convicted by Pilate on a civil charge, played right into God's hands. God would carry the world's condemnation through his Son's cross, and thus die to sin and death and condemnation on behalf of all humanity. He became our curse (Gal 3:13). That is how he saved the world. He did it because he loves the world—the whole beautiful, terrible, holy, cancerous, hilarious, reptilian, awful, and wonderful ball of wax (Jn 3:16–17). Leave it to God to die so well.

If you have read about a Jesus who says No to family and friends, if you have read about a Jesus who checks out all the time, if you have read about a Jesus who disturbs the peace on purpose, and if you have read about a Jesus unplugged from religious games and religious hype, and you are not ashamed of what you have read, then perhaps the kingdom has come near to you. Perhaps you have found your passion for the pearl. Maybe the seed scattered by that crazy farmer has finally fallen on good soil. Maybe it is time to party with the bridegroom.

Finally, if you have heard *Messiah damned* proclaimed in these pages, and it has not offended you, then you are blessed, for you have grasped that the power of God is in the weakness of his suffering, and the wisdom of God is in his foolish choice to die.

"Worthy is the Lamb that was slaughtered to receive power and wealth and wisdom and might and honor and glory and blessing!" (Rv 5:12, NRSV).

"And blessed is the one who is not offended by me" (Mt 11:6, ESV).

11

AN EPILOGUE FOR THE CHURCH

*"With every act of true proclamation, there also exists
the probability of persecution. Throughout the history
of the church, the stronger the Christian witness,
the greater the forces of oppression arrayed
against the witness."* [1]

—Randall Bush

There is a widespread belief that disturbances in the congregation are bad. "If we do *anything*," one staff parish committee chair said, "that causes one family to leave this church, it is wrong." This is the guiding philosophy in so many churches. It never seems to occur to anyone that what it means is that we must work very hard at doing nothing! Why not go ahead and post it on the church Web site and spell it out on the church street sign: *Murky Muck Memorial United Methodist Church: Where we make sure that nothing happens!*

If the Church Fails to Risk

Any Christian and any church that make a difference will cause a disturbance. It is unavoidable. And few consider Jesus's own command to make a difference, and not pull any punches. We are not supposed to privately repress secrets, but expose them. We are not supposed to stay home and play it safe, but go out there and tell it like it is. We will pay a price for doing this, but our cross is something we are supposed to be carrying anyway.

Here is the result of our failure. We have in too many places become "peace mongers."[2] We care more about peace than progress. We care more about togetherness than making a difference. We care more about good feelings than fulfilling our commission. As a result, we are stuck. We are afraid to do something, especially something significant. What will people say around town? What will the Baptists and Presbyterians think? What will our district superintendent and bishop do? What will Mr. Quitandtakemymoneywithme do? And we end up paralyzed and whining that every time the water gets stirred, someone else gets in before us. Thirty-eight years of paralysis. Thirty-eight years of doing nothing. Thirty-eight years of blaming the circumstances. Thirty-eight years of whining. That is what togetherness costs.

Another result is that we are held hostage. "Why is it that so many times it is the bullies who are running our churches?"[3] This was asked of an elderly ladies' Sunday School class. The pastor repeated the question. "How come belligerent, hotheaded, immature people are calling the shots in so many churches?" There was much silence and concern. The class members were anxious, and probably resentful that such a thing could be brought up and discussed in the Lord's House. After a moment, one of the feistier of the bunch spoke up and answered the question as well as it could be answered. She replied, "They run things because the rest of us just sit back with our arms folded and say, 'Whatever,' because we haven't got the guts to stand up to them."

She was right. The problem is not that bullies are so strong; it is that congregations are so weak. A common cold can take over the human body, if the body is weak. If the immune system has failed, any little old germ or bug can take over and even kill you.

When a bully threatens to quit and take his money if he does not get his way, then the message is clear and simple. The bully is making the price of his inclusion that he gets to call all the shots.[4] My dictionaries define that as *extortion*.

The woman from Sunday school class was absolutely right. We think disturbances are bad, so we let bad people run (and *ruin*) our churches! We let them have their way for the sake of *appearing* to be a peaceful congregation.

Think about it: Groups that focus on togetherness give strength to extremists—those willing to extort others.[5] And the tragedy is that when we get in this fix, we will likely blame and hate the bully/extremist for years. We will say nasty things about him over coffee and tell jokes on him at church socials. But the tragedy here is that we are not kidnapped against our will. We are hostages by choice! It is not the bully's fault. It is *our* fault. We would rather let a mean-spirited intimidator continue to push us around than to stand up to him and risk a scene.

Winston Churchill understood this. He explained the rise of Nazi Germany in Europe this way: "The malice of the wicked was reinforced by the weakness of the virtuous."[6] In other words, the Nazis drew their power from the spinelessness of the rest of Europe.

Churchill also said, "An appeaser is one who feeds the crocodile hoping it will eat him last."[7] Why do Christians and our churches continue to feed these crocodiles? Does no one realize that the crocs enjoy this? They love it! They love what they do. They love the notoriety and attention. And they often get their way. *And we let them.*

So how do we fix this? How do we get unstuck, and how do we handle the bullies running things? The answer is simple. Here it is. Ready? This is it: *Stand.* Do like Jesus and *stand.* How? Well, it is pretty easy, actually. It is the fallout that is hard. All you have to do is approve something. Approve buying a new parsonage. Approve knocking out a wall for a bigger nursery. Approve new drapes and carpet for the pastor's

residence. Approve moving the offertory to after the sermon
in the order of worship. Anything. It does not matter what.
Make some progress. Move ahead. The bully (or bullies) will
complain because the initiative did not come from him. And
when he complains, even if he throws a full-blown, red-faced,
screaming-and-slobbering tantrum, tell him firmly, politely,
"No, we are going to do this. You are welcome to participate,
but this action does not require your approval. If you can't
participate, we will be sorry, but we will understand." Then
if he threatens to leave and take his large family and their
money with him, ask him to stay, but hold the door for him
politely if he chooses to leave.

Now ... if you happen to be the pastor that pulls this off,
be prepared to search for a new church within the year. "No
good deed goes unpunished."[8] Our crucified Lord demonstrates this truth as no one and nothing else can.

Unplug Your Mind: How much is togetherness costing your
church?

If the Church Refuses to Die ...

It still seems that on planet earth, truly no good deed goes unpunished! Good is beset with sabotage. The greater the good,
the more intense the efforts to thwart. There is an alarming
and absolutely vital implication here for the church.

This next sentence is a lie, so please read it with as much
sarcasm as you can muster: "It is common knowledge that
successful pastors don't have unhappy parishioners."[9] As a
pastor, I thank you for reading that with sarcasm! Yet is this
not what lay people too often assume about ministers and
priests and rabbis, that things are going well when no one, or
at least very few, are upset? Is this not what clergy often assume about one another, that if one is keeping things stable
and even-keeled that one is a success, whatever that means?
Is this not what episcopal and ecclesiastical leaders too often

assume in the evaluation of the pastors they supervise and appoint: that if there are no complaints, then the appointment is going well, and conversely that if there are complaints, then it is not? Does not practically everyone assume that if the pastor is doing a good job, then the church membership *must* by definition be "happy"?

There is something very wrong with this picture. To make these assumptions, we would also have to assume that making everyone happy was *Jesus's* first priority, and that *he* upset no one. Was people-pleasing his priority? Did he avoid upsetting people? If so, then we have to assume that making everyone happy is the intent of the Gospel.

As we have seen, however, this cannot be. Jesus said he came not to bring peace but a sword. The Gospel divides people. Parables were told on purpose to disturb and sift. Jesus's conduct and message enraged people. They killed him for it. This has important implications for pastors and parishioners.

Where it is believed that successful pastoral leadership is defined by the happiness or unhappiness of parishioners, strong leadership is undercut, prophetic preaching is silenced, innovative ministry is sabotaged, and peace mongering, play-it-safe pastors are rewarded with promotion. In a nutshell, the herd is feeding its strongest to the crocodiles to appease them. The result is a weaker and weaker herd, and stronger and stronger crocs.

Where it is believed that successful churches are conflict-free, it is the extremists who are strengthened. Knowing that conflict will be avoided at all costs, knowing that most parishioners will cave in just to keep the peace, the extremists will consistently get their way. The result is that the crocs get stronger, and the herd is thinned out, paralyzed with fear, unwilling to risk.

Oh God, who will save us from this body of sin and death? (based on Rom 7:24).

Hear the words of Jesus: "No one takes [my life] from me, but I lay it down of my own accord. I have power to lay it down, and I have power to take it up again. I have received this command from my Father" (Jn 10:18, NRSV).

Shall we deny the power of the cross? Shall we act as though it never happened, that it has no power at all?

We are challenged to believe in the power of the cross; to take stands; to speak the truth; to expose the lies; to challenge hypocrites; to act in obedience to God; to then expect the attack, the ridicule, the sabotage, and whatever may come; to trust that in the death and resurrection of Jesus is the power not only to stand, but to endure the consequence of doing so; to be given by the Holy Spirit the power to endure, to persevere; to receive the gifts of tenacity, stick-to-it-iveness, resilience, persistence, and stamina; to believe that God has not given us a burden that we cannot bear; to be able to say: *No one takes my life either. I give it of my own accord. And the same power that Jesus had to give his life and take it up again will be given to me as well!*

Ponder for a moment what it might be like to follow Jesus and forget respect and acceptance and power. For that to happen, of course, Christians (and churches) would have to give away their reputations, their popularity, and in the end their very lives, just as he did. But by definition, is not that what we should be doing anyway, if we are really serious about following Jesus? Ponder what it might mean for us to abandon the respectable thing for the right thing.

Winston Churchill said, "People who are not prepared to do the unpopular things and defy the clamor of the multitudes are not fit to be ministers in times of difficulty."[10] To put it differently, *strong* leaders do not need to be liked.

A strong leader does not obsess about looking respectable, nice, or presentable. A strong leader does not obsess about propriety, popularity, or prestige. A strong leader does not coddle or cater to whiners, naysayers, and extortionists. Anyone who does not understand these things has not yet understood Jesus, his ministry, his teaching, or the power of the foolish, scandalous cross.

What is the implication for a church that would follow a crucified Christ—a God-damned Messiah who scandalizes and offends? We are contemplating, of all things, the death of the church. With all the energy going into church growth programs and stewardship gimmicks, the last thing you would think the church would consider is its own death. Who can deny that we have become obsessed with money and membership? Who can deny that we are afraid of conflict, and are cowered by bullies? Who can deny the hypocrisy?

Jesus did not call the church to be successful, nor did he call it to survive. Nor is it his will that we should to be held hostage by fear or intimidation.

The church of Jesus Christ is called to bravely put its life on the line.

That of course means standing, turning the other cheek, speaking the truth, and carrying the cross. In him we are anointed. In him we are crucified. Because of that, the church can say to hell with being respectable, nice, and presentable. To hell with propriety, popularity, and prestige. Church members, especially you leaders and pastors, are called to surrender your reputation at the door. You are called to abandon all self-salvation and self-promotion schemes. Throw it all back into the fiery pit of hell from whence it came and follow the raw-nerve, provocative Jesus of the New Testament gospels.

Only a dead church can hope for resurrection. Only a crucified church will be raised. New life will come to the church, but only if she dies. Only those who know they are blind can see. Only those who know they are lost are found. Only those who know they are dead are raised to new life.

Yes, it is scary. We should all be terrified. From the cup Jesus drank, we are called to drink. And if it is his will that this cup not pass, then his will be done.

William Wallace's prayer from his jail cell in *Braveheart,* could be our prayer, the church's prayer: *"Give us the strength to die well."*

Unplug Your Mind: How could the church change?

The Future of Evangelism

What are the two primary "evangelistic tools" in the church today? They are two sides of the same coin.

On the one side, threat: The church continues resorting to getting more members and money by trying to pressure people to the altar. The assumption is that no one will actually *want* to come of their own free will. That is why we pay the preacher to scare and threaten! To get more money and members, we must make them afraid of what might happen if they do not go to church. Guilt and shame them. Manipulate their emotions. Bring up the law. Accuse and condemn them. Intimidate them with what could happen to them on the way home. Tell them they will be punished.

On the other side, seduction: The church continues resorting to putting niceness, presentability, and respectability before all else—the belief being that if we gussie ourselves up and create a conflict-free facade, they will come. We will have special programs. We will fund state-of-the-art facilities. We will invite TV personalities. Visitors will say, *What a nice place. What nice people. Everything is so presentable and respectable. Everything is so cleancut and wholesome. Everything is so attractive, and entertaining too!* But will anyone think to ask, "Was the offensive Gospel preached?"

The church, it seems, does not trust the message of a mysterious kingdom. Maybe the church has lost its faith in the power of the cross. We seem to have concluded that the content of the Gospels is simply too abrasive, too outrageous, too unpleasant, too demanding, too foolish, and too offensive.

If we explain to people what the Gospels *really* say, we are afraid they will not come back.

Unplug Your Mind: Is there a better way to reach the world than seduction or threat?

Conclusion

When did this happen? Did the church just sit down one day and decide that it no longer had enough confidence in the Gospel to draw people to church? Did they vote one day to stop preaching and teaching the mysterious kingdom and the offensive cross? Did they study up on how to increase membership without having to tell anyone what Jesus *really* did and said? Who came up with the idea to scare people to church? Who came up with the idea to lure them to church? Hoping that people might come of their own free will to hear a not-so-nice, not-so-presentable, not-so-respectable Gospel must have somewhere been deemed too risky in terms of membership and money. Someone must have decided that scaring and luring would work better.

However, we might be bold and take a chance. What if we forget about frightening people to the altar, forget about enticing people onto the membership rolls, and return to the original plan? The biblical plan. We could join Matthew, Mark, Luke, John, and Paul in offering them Jesus uncensored, unedited, and unplugged.

APPENDIX 1
LISTING OF BIBLE TRANSLATIONS
USED IN *JESUS UNPLUGGED*

In crafting *Jesus Unplugged* the author uses several Bible translations. Typically information on the various translations are listed on the copyright page. Because several are used in this book we have chosen to list them here.

ESV   English Standard Version
        Wheaton: Crossway Books/Good News Publishers, 2001
NAB   The New American Bible
        Washington, D.C.: Confraternity of Christian Doctrine, 1991
NAS   The New American Standard Bible
        La Habra: The Lockman Foundation, 1995
NEB   The New English Bible: With the Apocrypha,
        Oxford Study Edition
        New York: Oxford University Press, 1976
NET   New English Translation, Dallas: Biblical Studies press,
        L.L. C. 1996–2005
NIV   The New International Version
        Colorado Springs: International Bible Society1984
NJB   The New Jerusalem Bible
        New York: Doubleday, 1985
NRSV   The New Revised Standard Version
        Grand Rapids: Zondervan,1989
RSV   Revised Standard Version
        New York: Oxford University Press,1973
TNIV   Today's New International Version.
        Colorado Springs: International Bible Society, 2005
YLT   The English Young's Literal Translation
        Ontario: Online Bible Foundation and Woodside
        Fellowship, 1988-1997

END NOTES

Chapter 1

1. Edwin H. Friedman, *Family Process and Process Theology—Video AL128* (Bethesda, MD: The Alban Institute, 1991).
2. Edwin H. Friedman, *Leadership Series—Audio* (Jackson, MS: St. Stephens Episcopal Church, 1991).
3. Edwin H. Friedman, *Live Lecture* (Decatur, IL: Decatur Presbyterian, 1995).
4. Edwin H. Friedman, *Leadership Series—Audio* (Jackson, MS: St. Stephens Episcopal Church, 1991).
5. Edwin H. Friedman, *Leadership Series—Audio* (Jackson, MS: St. Stephens Episcopal Church, 1991).
6. John J. Pilch, "Illuminating the World of Jesus through Cultural Anthropology." *The Living Light*, 31 January 1994, pp. 20–31. This article is a revision of a major address, "The Cultural World of Jesus," delivered at the Second Annual National Directors of Religious Education Convocation, April 6–9, 1994, in Anaheim, CA. It was updated for the following website on August 17, 1999: http://www.georgetown.edu/faculty/pilchj/CultJesus.htm

Chapter 2

1. Edwin H. Friedman, *Live Lecture* (Decatur, IL: Decatur Presbyterian, 1995).
2. Kenneth E. Bailey, *Through Peasant Eyes, A Literary-Cultural Approach to the Parables in Luke*, (Grand Rapids, MI: Wm. B. Eerdmans Publishing Company, 1976), p. 24.
3. James Fleming, A series of lectures on Jesus and his Jewish origins given at the Mississippi Annual Conference of The United Methodist Church in 1989 (Jackson, MS: Mississippi Annual Conference, 1989).
4. Tim Rice and Andrew Lloyd Weber, *Jesus Christ Superstar*, Original Broadway Cast Recording (New York, NY: Decca, 1971).
5. Fred B. Craddock, *Luke's Portrait of Jesus—Video* (Lubbock, TX: Net Video, 1988).

Chapter 3

1. Rami Arav and John J. Rousseau, *Jesus and His World: An Archaeological and Cultural Dictionary* (Minneapolis, MN: Fortress Press, 1995), pp. 214–216.
2. Gail R. O'Day, *The Gospel Of John, Volume Nine, The New Interpreter's Bible* (Nashville, TN: Abingdon Press, 1995), p. 536–537.

Chapter 4

1. Frederick Zugibe, (chief medical examiner of Rockland County, New York). It is well known, and there have been many cases of it. The clinical term is hematohidrosis. http://www.christiananswers.net/q-eden/edn-t018.html.

Chapter 5

1. Jerome Murphy-O'Connor, *The Holy Land, Oxford Archaeological Guides* (Oxford: Oxford University Press, 1998), pp. 28–29; and Charles R. Page II, *Jesus and the Land* (Nashville, TN: Abingdon Press, 1995), pp. 33–38.
2. Bruce M. Metzger, *A Textual Commentary on the Greek New Testament*. (London: United Bible Societies, Corrected Edition, 1975), p. 209.
3. Jerome Murphy-O'Connor, *The Holy Land, Oxford Archaeological Guides* (Oxford: Oxford University Press, 1998), pp. 28–29; and Charles R. Page II, *Jesus and the Land* (Nashville, TN: Abingdon Press, 1995), pp. 33–38.

Chapter 6

1. R.C.H. Lenski, *The Interpretation of St. Mark's and St. Luke's Gospels* (Columbus, OH: Lutheran Book Concern, 1934); and Timothy and Barbara Friberg, *Analytical Lexicon to the Greek New Testament* (Grand Rapids, MI: Baker Book House, 1994, 2000).

Chapter 7

1. Edwin H. Friedman, *Friedman's Fables* (New York, NY: The Guilford Press, 1990), pp. 9–13.

2. Edwin H. Friedman, *Generation to Generation: Family Process in Church and Synagogue* (New York, NY: The Guilford Press, 1985).

Chapter 8

1. Edwin H. Friedman, Live Lecture, (Decatur, IL: Decatur Presbyterian, 1995).

Chapter 9

1. Paul MacLean, *The Triune Brain* (New York, NY: Plenum Publishing Corporation, 1990), and the following websites: www.salesbrain.net/pages/references_resources.htm; www.terrybragg.com/Article_Reptilianbrain.htm
2. Edwin H. Friedman, Live Lecture (Decatur, IL: Decatur Presbyterian, 1995).

Chapter 10

1. Martin Hengel, *Crucifixion in the Ancient World and the Folly of the Message of the Cross* (Minneapolis, MN: Augsburg Fortress Publishers, 1977).
2. Edwin H. Friedman, *Leadership Series, Audio* (Jackson, MS: St. Stephens Episcopal Church, 1991).
3. Edwin H. Friedman, *Leadership Series, Audio* (Jackson, MS: St. Stephens Episcopal Church, 1991).
4. Edwin H. Friedman, *Leadership Series, Audio* (Jackson, MS: St. Stephens Episcopal Church, 1991).
5. Robert Farrar Capon, *Kingdom, Grace, Judgment: Paradox, Outrage, and Vindication in the Parables of Jesus.* (Grand Rapids, MI: Wm. B. Eerdmans Publishing Company, 2002).

Chapter 11

1. G. Lloyd Rediger, quotes Dr. Randall Bush, Professor of Christian Studies and Philosophy, Union University, Jackson, Tennessee, in "Clergy Killers," *The Clergy Journal*, August 1993, (Posted on the World Wide Web at http://jmm.aaa.net.au/articles/8591.htm).
2. Edwin H. Friedman, *Leadership Series, Audio* (Jackson, MS: St. Stephens Episcopal Church, 1991).

3. Edwin H. Friedman, *Leadership Series, Audio* (Jackson, MS: St. Stephens Episcopal Church, 1991).

4. Edwin H. Friedman, *Leadership Series, Audio* (Jackson, MS: St. Stephens Episcopal Church, 1991).

5. Edwin H. Friedman, *Leadership Series, Audio* (Jackson, MS: St. Stephens Episcopal Church, 1991).

6. Winston S. Churchill, *The Second World War, Volume 1: The Gathering Storm* (London: Mariner Books, Reissue Edition, 1986).

7. James C. Humes, *The Wit and Wisdom of Winston Churchill: A Treasury of More Than 1,000 Quotations and Anecdotes* (New York, NY: HarperPerennial, 1994), p. 7.

8. Clare Boothe Luce, *Quotes from Clare Boothe Luce* at http://www.cblpolicyinstitute.org/luce.htm, The Clare Boothe Luce Policy Institute.

9. G. Lloyd Rediger, "Clergy Killers," *The Clergy Journal*, August 1993 (Posted on the World Wide Web at http://jmm.aaa.net.au/articles/8591.htm).

10. James C. Humes, *The Wit and Wisdom of Winston Churchill: A Treasury of More Than 1,000 Quotations and Anecdotes* (New York, NY: HarperPerennial, 1994), p. 51.

BIBLIOGRAPHY

Arav, Rami, and Rousseau, John J. *Jesus and His World: An Archaeological and Cultural Dictionary*. Minneapolis: Fortress Press, 1995.

Bailey, Kenneth E. *Poet and Peasant AND Through Peasant Eyes, A Literary-Cultural Approach to the Parables in Luke, Combined Edition Two Volumes in One*. Grand Rapids, MI: Wm. B. Eerdmans Publishing Company, 1976.

Brown, Raymond E. *The Gospel According to John, 2 Volumes, The Anchor Bible*. Garden City, NJ: Doubleday & Company, Inc., 1966.

Buttrick, George Author, Editor. *The Interpreter's Dictionary of the Bible*. Nashville, TN: Abingdon Press, 1962.

Capon, Robert Farrar. *Kingdom, Grace, Judgment: Paradox, Outrage, and Vindication in the Parables of Jesus*. Grand Rapids, MI: Wm. B. Eerdmans Publishing Company, 2002.

Churchill, Winston S. *The Second World War, Volume 1: The Gathering Storm*. London: Mariner Books, Reissue Edition, 1986.

Craddock, Fred B. *John Knox Preaching Guides*. Atlanta, GA: John Knox Press, 1982.

Craddock, Fred B. *Luke, Interpretation: A Bible Commentary for Teaching and Preaching*. Louisville, KY: John Knox Press, 1990.

Craddock, Fred B. *Luke's Portrait of Jesus (video)*. Lubbock, TX: Net Video, 1988.

Fitzmyer, Joseph A. *The Gospel According to Luke, 2 Volumes, The Anchor Bible*. Garden City, NJ: Doubleday & Company, Inc., 1981.

Fleming, James. *A series of lectures on Jesus and his Jewish origins given at the Mississippi Annual Conference in 1989*. Jackson, MS: Mississippi Annual Conference, 1989.

Friberg, Timothy and Barbara. *Analytical Lexicon to the Greek New Testament*. Grand Rapids, MI: Baker Book House, 1994, 2000.

Friedman, Edwin H. *Family Process and Process Theology Video AL128*. Bethesda, MD: The Alban Institute, 1991.

Friedman, Edwin H. *A Failure of Nerve: Leadership in the Age of the Quick Fix, An Edited Manuscript*. Bethesda, MD, 1999.

Friedman, Edwin H. *Friedman's Fables*. New York, NY: The Guilford Press, 1990.

Friedman, Edwin H. *Generation to Generation: Family Process in Church and Synagogue*. New York, NY: The Guilford Press, 1985.

Friedman, Edwin H. *Leadership Series, Audio*. Jackson, MS: St. Stephens Episcopal Church, 1991.

Friedman, Edwin H. *Live Lecture*. Decatur, IL: Decatur Presbyterian, 1995.

Hengel, Martin. *Crucifixion in the Ancient World and the Folly of the Message of the Cross*. Minneapolis, MN: Augsburg Fortress Publishers, 1977.

Humes, James C. *The Wit and Wisdom of Winston Churchill: A Treasury of More Than 1,000 Quotations and Anecdotes*. New York: HarperPerennial, 1994.

Kittel, Gerhard, Editor. *Theological Dictionary of the New Testament, X Volumes*. Grand Rapids, MI: Wm. B. Eerdmans Publishing Company, 1964.

Kruger, C. Baxter. *Across All Worlds: Jesus Inside Our Darkness*. Jackson, MS: Perichoresis Press, 2005.

Kruger, C. Baxter. *Jesus and the Undoing of Adam*. Jackson, MS: Perichoresis Press, 2003.

Lenski, R.C.H. *The Interpretation of St. Mark's and St. Luke's Gospels*. Columbus, OH: Lutheran Book Concern, 1934.

Louw, J. P. and Nida, E. A., Editors. *Louw-Nida Greek-English Lexicon of the New Testament Based on Semantic Domains, 2nd Edition*. New York, NY: United Bible Societies, 1988.

Luce, Clare Boothe. Quotes from Clare Boothe Luce at http://www.cblpolicyinstitute.org/luce.htm, The Clare Boothe Luce Policy Institute.

Matthews, Victor H. *Manners and Customs in the Bible: An Illustrated Guide to Daily Life in Bible Times*. Peabody, MA: Hendrickson Publishers, Third Printing Revised Edition, 1993.

MacLean, Paul. *The Triune Brain*. New York, NY: Plenum Publishing Corporation, 1990. (and the following websites: http://www.salesbrain.net/pages/references_resources.htm; http://www.terrybragg.com/Article_Reptilianbrain.htm)

Metzger, Bruce M. *A Textual Commentary on the Greek New Testament*. London: United Bible Societies, Corrected Edition, 1975.

Murphy-O'Connor, Jerome. *The Holy Land, Oxford Archaeological Guides*. Oxford: Oxford University Press, 1998.

Newman, Jr., Barclay M. *A Concise Greek-English Dictionary of the New Testament*. New York, NY: United Bible Societies, 1971

O'Day, Gail R. *The Gospel Of John, Volume Nine, The New Interpreter's Bible*. Nashville, TN: Abingdon Press, 1995. (Jesus calls her "Woman" pp. 536–537)

Page II, Charles R. *Jesus and the Land*. Nashville, TN: Abingdon Press, 1995. (Nazareth stuff pp. 33–38)

Page II, Charles R., and Voltz, Carl A. *The Land and the Book: An Introduction to the World of the Bible*. Nashville, TN: Abingdon Press, 1993. (Nazareth stuff on p. 162)

Pilch, John J. "Illuminating the World of Jesus Through Cultural Anthropology." *The Living Light* 31/1 (1994) 20–31. This article is a revision of a major address, "The Cultural World of Jesus," delivered at the Second Annual National Directors of Religious Education Convocation, April 6–9, 1994, in Anaheim, CA. It was updated for the following website on August 17, 1999: http://www.georgetown.edu/faculty/pilchj/CultJesus.htm

Pixner, Bargil. *With Jesus in Jerusalem: His First and Last Days in Judah*. Rosh Pina, Israel: Corazin Publishing, 1996.

Pixner, Bargil. *With Jesus Through Galilee According to the Fifth Gospel*. Rosh Pina, Israel: Corazin Publishing, 1992.

Rediger, G. Lloyd, "Clergy Killers." *The Clergy Journal*: August 1993 (posted on the World Wide Web at http://jmm.aaa.net.au/articles/8591.htm)

Rice, Tim, and Weber, Andrew Lloyd. *Jesus Christ Superstar: Original Broadway Cast Recording*. New York, NY: Decca, 1971.

Zeitlin, Irving M. *Jesus and the Judaism of His Time*. Cambridge: Polity Press, 1988.

Zugibe, Frederick (Chief medical examiner of Rockland County, New York). On the World Wide Web at http://www.christiananswers.net/q-eden/edn-t018.html.

SCRIPTURE INDEX

Chapter 7
Page 112
Mt 25:1–13
Page 115
Mt 28:19
Page 117
Mk 13:10
Page 118
Mt 13:35
Mk 4:33–34
Mt 13:11–12
Page 119
Mt 13:13–15
Is 6:9
Lk 17:20–21
Mt 13:1–9
Mt 13:31–21
Mt 13:33
Mt 13:34
Page 120
Mt 13:35–36
Mt 13:47–48
Lk 17:20–21
Mt 9:14–15
Page 121
Lk 19:41–48
Jn 9:39–41
Jn 9:24
Mt 11:9
Jn 8:48
Mk 3:21
Mt 13:10
Page 122
Mt 6:10
Lk 11:2
Mt 22:23–33
Lk 16:19–31
Jn 14:2
Lk 23:43

Page 123
1 Cor 15:42–44
Jn 10:10b
Page 124
1Jn 4:8, 16
1 Jn 4:18
Page 126
Jn 12:47b
Jn 5:45
Gal 3:24
Page 127
Gal 3:10
Jn 5:45
Chapter 8
Page 128
Lk 7:31–34
Lk 13:1–5
Lk 7:31–35
Page 129
Lk 7:32
Lk 7:33–34
Lk 7:35
Jn 8:43–44
Page 130
Lk 7:31–34
Page 131
Jn 5:6–7
Lk 12:13
Page 132
1Kgs 19:9–10
Jb2:7–9
Gn 3:11–13
Lk 7:32
Page 133
Jn 3:19
Jn 10:18
Page 134
Lk 13:1

Page 135
Mt 22:15–22
Lk 13:1–5
Chapter 9
Page 139
Mt 5:39
Page 141
Jn 18:5
Page 142
Jn 18:4–8
Lk 22:52–53
Mt 26:36–58
Mk 14:32–50
Lk 22:39–54
Jn 18:1–14
Jn 18:20–21
Jn 18:22
Jn 18:23
Page 143
Is 31:4
Mt 11:29
Jn 17:24
Page 144
Lk 14:25–33
Page 145
Mt 10:37
Mt 10:21–22
Mt 10:16–36
Page 147
Mt 10:16–39
Lk 4:28–30
Mk 5:17
Page 148
Lk 12:2
Lk 12:49
Mi 7:2
Mt 10:36
Mt 12:48
Mk 3:33

ABOUT THE AUTHOR

Bert Gary is a writer, pastor, and lecturer. He taught regularly in Israel between 1994 and 2001 and has since taught in Turkey and Greece. For eleven years he directed and taught in two United Methodist graduate programs for local pastors for the Jerusalem Institute for Biblical Exploration (formerly the Jerusalem Center for Biblical Studies) and for Candler School of Theology at Emory University. He has degrees in theology, psychology, and music from Emory.

Bert has begun his twentieth year of ordained ministry and currently lives in Florence, Mississippi with his wife, Kathy, where he is the pastor of Marvin United Methodist Church. He has three children ages 20, 17, and 14; three grown stepchildren; and two step-grandsons.

Among Bert's other passions are archaeology, music, and ornithology.